RECONSTRUCTING BEIRUT

JAMAL AND RANIA DANIEL SERIES
*in Contemporary History, Politics,
Culture, and Religion of the Levant*

RECONSTRUCTING BEIRUT

Memory and Space in a Postwar Arab City

ASEEL SAWALHA

UNIVERSITY OF TEXAS PRESS

Austin

Requests for permission to reproduce material from this work should
be sent to:
    Permissions
    University of Texas Press
    P.O. Box 7819
    Austin, TX 78713-7819
    www.utexas.edu/utpress/about/bpermission.html

⊗ The paper used in this book meets the minimum requirements of
ANSI/NISO Z39.48-1992 (R1997) (Permanence of Paper).

LIBRARY OF CONGRESS CATALOGING-IN-PUBLICATION DATA

Sawalha, Aseel, 1966-
Reconstructing Beirut : memory and space in a postwar Arab city /
Aseel Sawalha. — 1st ed.
p. cm. — (Jamal and Rania Daniel series in contemporary history,
politics, culture, and religion of the Levant)
Includes bibliographical references and index.
ISBN 978-0-292-72881-3
1. Urban renewal—Lebanon—Beirut. 2. City planning—Lebanon—
Beirut—History—20th century. 3. Lebanon—Economic conditions—
1990- I. Title.
HT169.L42B482 2010
307.3′40956925—dc22

                                                        2009041323

*To my parents
and all the residents of wounded Arab cities*

CONTENTS

A NOTE ON LANGUAGE

To transliterate Arabic words, I have used a modified version of the *International Journal of Middle East Studies* (*IJMES*). Some of the Arabic words are transliterated using the classical Arabic; others are transliterated using the Lebanese Arabic dialect. Arabic words commonly used in English are spelled the way they appear in English publications (e.g., Hizballah). For the sake of simplicity and clarity, I did not do literal translation.

Except for public figures, I changed the names of individuals unless otherwise noted.

ACKNOWLEDGMENTS

This book would not have been possible without the support, guidance, and hospitality of friends and colleagues across multiple cities and spaces. Here I will be able to mention some names, while many others need to remain anonymous.

Starting with the CUNY Graduate Center, I would like to thank my dissertation committee, especially Vincent Crapanzano, my advisor and mentor. I will always be indebted to his inspiring ideas, encouragement, and belief that the project would get done even when my field data seemed lost. Conversations with him opened new intellectual horizons. Setha Low led me to view the "urban" with different eyes. Her innovative ideas on spatial analysis and her "Anthropology of Space and Place" meetings provided the conceptual atlas that guided my thinking through the chaos of postwar Beirut. Talal Asad enriched my understanding of anthropological theories and provided a mind-opening interpretation of the Middle East. Finally, Robert Fernea stepped up at the eleventh hour to serve as my outside examiner and offered thoughtful responses to the work.

In the Department of Anthropology at CUNY Graduate Center, I would like to extend my thanks to all the faculty members, especially Louise Lennihan, Leith Mullings, Jane Schnider, and Neil Smith, with special gratitude to the cheerful effectiveness of the Assistant Program Officer, Ellen DeRiso. The camaraderie of Molly Doane, Hugo Benavides, Murphy Halliburton, Carmen Medeiros, Kee Yong, Julia Butterfield, Bea Vidacs, Yvonne LaSalle, Charles Price, Laure Bjawi, Ara Wilson, and Arlene Davila lightened my journey through graduate school and the junior-faculty stage.

At Pace University, I would like to extend my gratitude for the encouragement and support of friends and colleagues I worked alongside while finishing this book: Roger Salerno, Denise Santiago, Amy Forester, Satish Kholluri, Karla Jay, Christopher Malone, Joseph Franco, Joan Roland, Joseph Lee, and the Dean of Dyson College, Nira Herrmann.

My former student Ashley Marinaccio kindly offered recent photographs of Lebanon, and Amina Chowdhury provided valuable data entry.

Numerous residents of Beirut whom I interviewed warmly opened their homes and shared their stories and memories, some of which must have been painful to recall. A number of these individuals evolved from anthropological interlocutors to lifelong friends.

Indispensable friends and colleagues in Beirut, in addition to their hospitality and lively discussions, helped in the difficult first steps of fieldwork by introducing me to their networks and facilitating interviews: Sameera Khouri, Kirstin Scheid, Mona Aboud, Edward El-Qash, Motaz Dajani, Huda Zurayk, Ikram Sharara, Rosemary Sayigh, Martha Mundy, Richard Smith, and Leila Hamdan. *Shukran jazeelan.*

Other friends and colleagues who were researching different projects in Beirut alongside me shared resources, intense conversation, and good times: Daniel Genberg, Mona Harb, Najib Hourani, Nakeema Stefflbauer, Lurie King, Maha Yahya, Yasmin Arif, Rola Majdalani, and Hasan Diab. I learned personal perspectives on Lebanon from other entertaining companions outside of research: Ahmad Salam, Rouane Itani, Zeina Shihab, and Zeynab Saqallah.

I owe thanks to institutions in Beirut, notably the American University of Beirut, where I was a visiting fellow at the Center for Behavioral Research, and where the chair, Samir Khalaf, and the graduate students Maysoon Sukareyeh, Zeina Misk, and Michelle Obeid were very helpful. Fawaz Traboulsi generously shared his extensive knowledge of the ins and outs of Lebanon, along with challenging questions. Jean Hannoyer, the director of the French Centre d'Etudes et de Recherches sur le Moyen-Orient Contemporain (CERMOC), welcomed me to their rich archive.

I cannot find the words to thank those who rescued my data when my fieldwork abruptly ended and who offered invaluable practical and emotional support: Kirstin Scheid, Samira Khouri, Motaz Dajani, May Hamdan, Khalil Mkari, and Maysoon Annahar. Bilal al-Amin always appeared at the right moment.

Extending further back in time, I am profoundly grateful to Seteney Shami, who introduced me to anthropological fieldwork as a graduate student at Yarmouk University, and who has continued to guide me along my path. From the end of my fieldwork onward, Kate Wilson has been by my side through all thick description.

I am indebted to colleagues in anthropology and Middle East studies beyond my own departments who generously provided comments, asked questions, and read part or all of the manuscript. Bassam Abed and Peter

Sieger witnessed this project from its inception; Julie Peteet offered intellectual and personal generosity; Lucine Taminian has shared journeys in Jordan, Beirut, and New York. I learned from friends who were also conference co-panelists: Rhodah Kanaaneh, Tom Abowd, Anny Bakalian, and Farha Ghannam. Ongoing dialogue with colleagues working on Lebanon—Sofian Merabet, Najib Hourani, Michael Gasper, Michael Davie, Michelle Obeid, and Mozna al-Masri—enriched my thinking about Beirut. Certain prominent Middle East specialists strengthened my foundations in the field: Leila Abu Lughod, Suad Joseph, Tim Mitchell, and Amal Rassam. Outside of academia, I have enjoyed conversations with two friends, Tamara al-Fadel and Denise Nassar, about their encounters with Lebanon.

The reviewers of the manuscript made insightful and valuable suggestions. My coach, the late Rose McAloon, was indispensable to the rewriting. My "writing days" with Andrea Flores-Khalil were helpful. In polishing the book, I am grateful to my editors, Jim Burr, Lynne Chapman, and Nancy Warrington, for strengthening the book with friendly efficiency.

The research for fieldwork and write-up was funded by the Middle East Awards from the Population Council, a Scholarly Research Grant from Pace University, and a CUNY Teaching Fellowship.

Finally, my parents' unwavering faith in education made this project possible; to them I dedicate the book. I also offer it on behalf of my siblings scattered across the Palestinian diaspora.

RECONSTRUCTING BEIRUT

INTRODUCTION

This book is an ethnographic study of time, place, and memory in the aftermath of the devastating civil war that ravaged Beirut, Lebanon, from 1975 to 1991. It focuses on the rebuilding efforts of the city and describes how the residents of Beirut used individual and collective memories of their celebrated architectural past to compete and negotiate for the reinstatement of municipal services and the reconstruction of their urban environment. It explores how ordinary citizens insisted that specific urban spaces be restored as they were recollected from before, during, and after the war. As it traces Beirutis' strategic attempts to exert influence over the rebuilding of their beloved city, this study investigates the struggles surrounding contradictory visions of public space, individual perceptions of time, and conflicting memories of the city's past. The theme of the memories of the city's past, a temporality of urban space, runs through all the chapters.

This study places Beirut's reconstruction project within the broader frame of emerging theories of globalization and political economy. It documents the city's transformation within the arc of its own history as well as that of the entire Middle East. The ethnographic data and theoretical analysis fall within the existing anthropological literature on place and space and memory and remembrance, which I review in the first chapter, giving the overview for the rest of the chapters, which are based on fieldwork case studies. Chapters Two to Six dwell on the postwar phase, while the afterword jumps forward to recent events.

In the first chapter, "Beirut: A City in Transition," I introduce Beirut's postwar physical, social, and political structures. My description includes my own challenges of gathering data in the midst of an unpredictable transitional postwar urban context. To sketch the context for this recent scenario, the chapter recounts how the sixteen-year Lebanese civil war (1975–1991), much of which was fought within Beirut's boundaries, drastically transformed the physical landscape of the city and destroyed much of its downtown area. From its former elegance, Beirut's center was reduced to a "ghost town."

This background section also recognizes that Beirut's physical destruction was accompanied by a massive demographic upheaval, as fully half of its population was uprooted and relocated to temporary quarters in abandoned apartments, hotels, and office buildings. Downtown Beirut, the former cosmopolitan showcase of the Arab world and the focus of this study, was all but destroyed. In addition to the physical destruction, the chapter also describes the societal upheaval as the institutions and services of the Lebanese state disappeared during the war, leaving political factions and militias to seize control and establish ad hoc, nonlegal systems of negotiating space and resources.

After this background, I shift my attention to the events that shaped the postwar rebuilding efforts. When the fighting officially ended in the early 1990s, the state sought to reinstate its legitimacy; restore a sense of normalcy; and begin the daunting task of rebuilding its capital, its institutions, and its infrastructure. The priority then became the reconstruction of Beirut's war-ravaged downtown area, commonly called "the heart of the city," to its former grandeur. In the proposed restoration plan, Beirut's center was envisioned as a "melting pot," where diverse sects and ideologies could interact peacefully and where Lebanon's eighteen ethno-religious groups could intermingle freely.

Chapter Two, "Downtown in 'the Ancient City of the Future,'" focuses on the monumental transformation of the heart of Beirut, the controversial development project designed to rebuild the decimated downtown district. Much of it centers on the role played by "Solidere,"[1] the private real estate company that Prime Minister Hariri entrusted to oversee the reconstruction. According to Solidere, the rebuilding of Beirut's Central District was the world's largest urban renewal effort of its time. However, its approach to the project provoked controversy and resistance across all sectarian divides. In Chapter Two, I consider the events from the perspective of the economically powerful and the political elite. I juxtapose Solidere's plans with the competing discourses of intellectuals, historians, urban planners, and social scientists surrounding the project, the voices in closest dialogue with it. These debates, while based on competing visions of concrete spaces, are also informed by perceptions of large concepts: the past, heritage, and identity. The conflicting interests of the various factions, and the vicissitudes of their efforts to exert influence on the renewal project, make up the core of this entire study. The ethnographic material throughout the book examines the multiple repercussions of Solidere's project on other, less powerful groups.

Since the reconstruction project was launched, official and popular discourse had insisted that the city's wartime divisions no longer existed. State policy after "the end of emergency" decreed a prompt return to "normality" and a desire to "put aside the mentality of the war." But, as I argue in this book, for the citizens of Beirut, the war was not yet over. I frame this limbo as an ongoing "state of emergency" and as perpetual uncertainty. The top-down imposition of reconstruction generated uncertainty that crossed all aspects of daily life for most residents of the city. After Chapter Two, each of the following chapters illustrates a postwar case of uncertainty. In particular, I present the efforts of Beirutis to counter the unpredictability in various ways. In the course of my research, I repeatedly heard Beirutis echo the phrase "let's wait and see." Leaving the elites and the macro view of the commercial district, I recount the effects of reconstruction on apartment buildings in an adjacent neighborhood, 'Ayn el-Mreisse. I describe the drastic and palpable transformations engendered by postwar reconstruction: old buildings being demolished, new buildings under construction, the eviction of long-standing tenants, and the disruption of long-established social networks. My case studies present longtime, legal apartment dwellers who responded to the uncertainty of their futures as tenants, and who plied various tactics to secure their homes—including using their past memories. Along with this medley of individual voices, I trace the alliances and conflicts among the major actors in this single neighborhood, especially landlords and their long-standing tenants whom they sought to evict. Not just local disputes, these apartment conflicts touched all the major postwar power actors: political parties, government institutions, and financial forces. The chapters' cases articulate their respective roles and their active strategies in shaping the future of the neighborhood.

The third and fourth chapters form a unit based on the same neighborhood. However, "Beirut Is Ours Not Theirs: Neighborhood Sites and Struggles in 'Ayn el-Mreisse" shifts from individual actors to organized groups, and from living spaces to more public sites, which provoked different strategies and negotiations. Specifically, I investigate how local residents challenged their exclusion from the reconstruction process and how they formed groups to negotiate for urban rights. Although the spaces in dispute were not homes, these groups, like the residential tenants, used their recollections of prewar and wartime experiences to justify their claim to particular city sites. The chapter explores four distinct cases. First, I recount the efforts of fishermen to protect the city's last fishing port, unique in this book as the only work space, and one associated with nature rather than cities. The quotation of the title, "Beirut Is Ours Not Theirs," in their case refers to a luxury condominium building planned for the port site, but the same oppositional mode colored the other cases as well. Next, I move to a battle between a house of worship and a nightclub, as the neighborhood mosque's committee strove to obstruct the opening of a Hard Rock Cafe franchise. After discussing those two long-existing sites, I move on to a new site established in reaction to the same threats, to the case of a single man who installed an improvised, eclectic museum to protect the local heritage. My final case looks at a more formal cultural venue, one with a changing identity. Rather than a new one like the museum, or a continual one like the port and the mosque, this case describes a theater that had been suspended during the war and that a committee was now working to convert into a different cultural locale, a cultural center.

In Chapter Five, "Cafés, Funerals, and the Future of Coffee Spaces," I leave the neighborhood examined in the last two chapters and shift to a new kind of site, the place where people drink coffee together. More drastically than the homes or the threatened places in the ʿAyn el-Mreisse, these coffee venues took different forms before, during, and after the war. In the main case study, I analyze the nostalgic narratives of middle-class women who before the war gathered to drink coffee in French-style cafés, then met in funeral homes during the war. However, in the aftermath of the war, the tourist and business orientation of development left them with no place to gather. Unlike in the previous chapter, where those who felt uncertain and threatened made efforts to protect or renovate existing spaces, these social coffee drinkers resorted only to memories of spaces now destroyed. The memories of middle-class women and working-class men help challenge the traditional binary analysis of public/private space that fills many writings on gender in the Middle East.

In the last chapter of the immediate postwar years, "Placing the War-Displaced," I turn to the most marginal, least powerful, but most discussed group: the population displaced by the war, most of whom had fled their homes and lived by squatting and informal labor in the capital, Beirut. I compare the self-perception of the displaced, contrast it to the discourse of landlords whose properties they had occupied, as well as the press, political parties, government agencies, and organizations that work with the displaced. Despite wide disagreement over how to define "displaced," all but the displaced themselves shared the view that they were a problem—unwanted reminders of the war who should return to their prewar homes. Three individual case studies illustrate the diversity and complexity within the displaced population, and their relationship to the past in negotiating homes in the current or future city.

I conclude with an afterword, "Reclaiming Downtown Again," which turns to the chain of disruptions that struck Beirut in 2005, when protesters took over the downtown district. Occupying the space in ways that contradicted the upscale design of reconstruction, they too invoked the past, although in a history updated to include the recent catastrophes, while simultaneously using a new kind of public space, the Internet.

The reconstruction project engendered a permeating sense of uncertainty and limbo that crossed most social groups and endured for at least a decade. I do not suggest that the "let's wait and see" attitude rendered Beirutis passive; on the contrary, I found them fully engaged in negotiating for their survival. Tenants, whether legal or "illegal," sought resources and strategies to hold on to or acquire living space; neighborhood residents resisted the imposition of top-down planning by various tactics, including improbable alliances. However, I also found that they regarded their present circumstance as a temporary phase to be endured until their lives resumed "normality." Property owners waited for the war refugees to vacate their homes and businesses and for the municipal government to restore the city's infrastructure. Displaced families negotiated for monetary compensation and legal leases while they referred often to their numbered position on the many "waiting lists."[2] And everyone eagerly awaited the promised rebirth of Beirut's center and its restoration to its prewar reputation as the "Paris of the Middle East." The book ultimately examines the social meaning of space in the context of the city's remembered past and in relation to particular people's identities. Through ethnographic data, each section explores the ways urban space is negotiated, recalled, and contested.

DISAPPEARING NEIGHBORHOODS

During my first trip to Beirut, in the summer of 1995, I chose the neighborhood of Zqaq el-Blāṭ as a fieldsite to conduct my research for a doctoral dissertation.[1] At that time, I believed Zqaq el-Blāṭ was an ideal site for anthropological inquiry for several reasons. It was one of the oldest and liveliest neighborhoods adjacent to the downtown area, then under construction. Its narrow streets were crowded with small shops and residential buildings, children played in the roads, old men sat in front of shops, and women sat on balconies overlooking the narrow alleys. When I returned to New York to write my proposal about the ways in which daily life in Zqaq el-Blāṭ was shaped by the reconstruction project, I presumed I had found an ideal fieldsite.

However, on my second visit to Beirut, six months later, the proposed research site looked like an abandoned Hollywood movie set. After the real estate and construction company Solidere took over a large part of the neighborhood, the majority of the area's residents had been evacuated; many of the buildings had been demolished, even though a few concrete skeletons of several buildings were designated as landmarks to be renovated and preserved; and a highway under construction had divided the neighborhood into two parts. The noise of bulldozers and trucks replaced the once-vibrant and vital life of the neighborhood's residents. The area was deserted except for construction workers and equipment. Because of this dramatic change in the physical appearance of the neighborhood, and because most of its residents had been expelled from their homes and businesses to make way for new buildings, Zqaq el-Blāṭ was no longer a valid anthropological fieldsite.

Similarly, the downtown area that had formerly been occupied by thousands of families displaced by the war was now virtually empty. Solidere, working with governmental agencies, evicted all the displaced people and later demolished most of the remaining buildings. Archaeologists[2] worked side by side with construction workers, bulldozers, and demolition equipment. Amid the rubble of destroyed buildings stood one renovated building that housed the offices of the reconstruction company, Solidere.

Within this context of instability and unpredictability, and, most importantly, because of the absence of any residents in the area, I had to choose another neighborhood as an alternative fieldsite. The neighborhood had to be close to the downtown area so that I could study the effects of the urban renewal project on the daily lives of local residents, and I hoped that the neighborhood would not disappear due to reconstruction. After visiting various areas and consulting with friends and colleagues also conducting research in the city, I decided to work in a neighborhood called 'Ayn el-Mreisse. One of the oldest neighborhoods in Beirut, it is located west of the downtown area and faces the Mediterranean. Its inhabitants belonged to various sectarian groups and classes who had settled in the area before, during, and after the war. 'Ayn el-Mreisse was also undergoing major changes. Investors bought old houses and buildings to start new international and regional businesses; landlords were faced with the decision of whether to sell their properties for high prices to investors and outsiders or to hold on to their buildings and preserve their neighborhood; the displaced and the long-standing tenants negotiated for compensation and sought out alternative housing options.

After I started my research in 'Ayn el-Mreisse, I realized that studying a single neighborhood did not encompass a broad enough area to reflect the major transformations that had taken place in Beirut in the postwar era of reconstruction. I also realized that to limit myself to one neighborhood would not yield a comprehensive analysis because the residents of 'Ayn el-Mreisse were not confined to their neighborhood in their daily lives. Instead, I found that they were connected through a set of complex social, economic, and political networks with other groups, individuals, and institutions within the city, the country, and even globally.

In view of that, my research transcended the limits of a single neighborhood, a particular ethnic or religious group, a socioeconomic class, or a single moment in time. Rather, I incorporated data about a number of neighborhoods, such as the Southern Suburb of Beirut al-Dahiyya, where many of the displaced families had moved, and other neighborhoods adjacent to 'Ayn el-Mreisse, such as the Hamra District, Ras Beirut, and Minat el-Husson, where local residents of 'Ayn el-Mreisse worked, shopped, and socialized. In contrast to the work of urban anthropologists who "locate their tribes within the city" (Mullings 1987), this project is not an ethnog-

A typical contrast between the decimated buildings in the foreground and the new sleek high-rise behind them

raphy of a single group or neighborhood; rather, it is an ethnography of multiple urban spaces and sites. I examine the ways spaces are used, negotiated, and remembered by various groups and individuals. My work examines a set of complex socioeconomic and political networks that move beyond ethnic and class boundaries and analyzes these networks within the city as well as their regional and international connections. Besides crossing space, my study crosses time, as I present the ways residents of the city talked about the past (prewar and wartime period), the present (postwar era of construction), and the future.

Throughout my fieldwork, I interviewed diverse groups and individuals from almost all sectors of Beirut, from ordinary citizens to government officials, religious to secular, informal groups to established institutions, crossing economic class and social status.

For the authorities' perspective on development, I spoke with representatives from the Council for Development and Reconstruction (CDR), the Municipality of Beirut, and the Ministry of Tourism. I gathered information about Solidere from interviews, visits to the office, their official tour, their print material, and their representation abroad. I also visited the offices of investors, developers, and relevant architectural firms. Exploring development's effects on residents' daily lives, on the other hand, brought me into contact with people and groups at very local levels. Chapters Two and Three incorporate interviews with apartment dwellers facing eviction, fishermen, mosque members, cultural organizers, and other residents. Some interlocutors were speaking individually, as were many tenants, while others represented local groups with varying degrees of formality. All through the study I invoke the political viewpoints of disbanded yet still lingering militias; active religious parties, especially the Amal Movement, but also its rival, Hizballah, and other Islamic groups; and secular political parties, both socialist and nationalist. Many of my informants spoke at the personal level, especially tenants and the displaced, though their stories usually echoed those of others like them. Other interviewees spoke on behalf of relatively small organizations, all responding to postwar problems: family organizations, Beirut the Heritage, the Association for the Rights of Property Owners, the Association for the Revival of the Heritage of 'Ayn el-Mreisse, the Mosque Committee, and the Beirut Theater Committee. My discussion of the displaced (Chapter Six) relied on conversations with officials at the Ministry of the Displaced and the Central Fund for the Displaced, as well as the displaced themselves from across the city, and, at the international level, the United Nations Development Program (UNDP). Most of these conversations are not limited to single chapters or sections, but rather interweave across multiple chapters. In combination, they offer multiple perspectives of Beirut, both its past and its contemporary state.

ANTHROPOLOGY OF SPACE AND PLACE

Influenced by Michel Foucault's proposition that space should not be treated as "dead, fixed, un-dialectical, and immobile" (1980, 70), socio-cultural studies have begun to theorize the complex relationship between space and time and then examine how space is produced by powerful actors to dominate, discipline, and control the less powerful. These writings draw on dichotomies of power such as strong-weak, rich-poor, colonizer-colonized, and government-governed. For example, in his book *The Practice of Everyday Life*, French sociologist Michel de Certeau distinguishes between the panoptic vision of urban planners and the responses of the "ordinary practitioners of the city whose bodies follow the thicks and thins of urban text without being able to read it" (1988, 93).

Other studies have looked at space as a locus of power and have examined the ways in which the colonizers controlled their subjects by reorganizing and reshaping local spaces (Foucault 1977b; Mitchell 1988; Wilson 1991; Wright 1991; Yiftachel 1995). Although colonial cities are often viewed as socially, racially, and culturally diverse, these cities are spatially segregated because the colonizers dominate the natives through urban planning. For example, in the city of Algiers, the French built a modern city on the outskirts of the old Algerian *qaṣba*, confining the locals to their old traditional quarters (Alsayyad 1992; King 1992; Yeoh 1996). Similar to the colonizers who practice their power through spatial control, in the period after colonization, local national governments adopted the same colonial methods and asserted their powers by carrying out major projects to restructure urban spaces (Ghannam 2002; Holston 1989; Ribeiro 1989, 1994).[3]

In my work, I investigate how political and economic elites' control of space underestimates the role of marginal groups in shaping and changing the meaning of urban space. Following Foucault's proposition that space is a "fundamental [factor] in any exercise of power" (1986, 252), some social theorists argue that the meaning of urban space is a result of the power relationships, practices, and identities of the "ordinary practitioners of the city" (Giddens 1987; Gustafson 2001; Healey 2004; Miles 1997; Pred 1984; Soja 1989). Furthermore, other theorists suggest that space is not merely a container for social relations, but that the social instead is spatially constructed (Cameron and Coafee 2005; Escobar 2001; Massey 1994). Geographer Don Mitchell, in his expansion on Henri Lefebvre's notion of the "right to the city," distinguished between planned, controlled, and ordered spaces, and places that are appropriated, lived in, used, and negotiated by those who are excluded from taking part in determining the future of their surrounding environment (2003).

In view of that, I suggest that because the spatial shapes socioeconomic and political networks, place becomes an important element in the formation of urban identities and loyalties. For example, in my work, the less powerful residents of postwar Beirut recall selective memories of places where they lived and socialized in order to negotiate legal urban rights. On a few occasions, these spatial memories and identities determined the future of contested urban sites. For instance, when Solidere drew up the plans to demolish the whole city center, local residents protested and claimed emotional and historical connections to specific buildings. As a compromise, Solidere modified its plans and promised to restore two hundred "historically valuable buildings."

Building on sociological and anthropological theories of place, my work about spatial experiences in Beirut introduces the concept of "prohibited space." By prohibited space, I mean urban sites that were originally "public" and within reach for the majority of the city residents but, because of the war and the various urban renewal projects, had become "private," that is, inaccessible and out of reach for the majority of the population. During the war, the "Green Line,"[4] or the no-man's-land, divided the war-torn city into two parts, West and East, Muslim and Christian. With rare exceptions, those who lived in one part of the city never crossed to the other part.

Accordingly, over the years, East Beirut became unfamiliar and inaccessible for most of those who lived in West Beirut, and vice versa. The part of the city where residents were not allowed to live or enter became prohibited and physically inaccessible. These prohibited places were transformed into sites of nostalgia and remembrance. When the war came to an end in 1991, many of the prohibited sites became accessible again, but they continued to be foreign and unfamiliar to those who lived on "one side" of the city and who paid cautious visits to the "other side." On my second visit to Beirut, in 1996, I accompanied a friend visiting from the United States to watch a film at a newly opened movie theater in East Beirut. Traveling to the "east side" during daytime was not a problem, but on the way back, it was almost impossible to convince a taxi driver to cross to the "other side." Finally, after offering to pay extra fees, a taxi driver agreed to take us to West Beirut. It was obvious that the driver was unfamiliar with the streets; he asked us "if we think it is safe over there these days." He said that he has fond memories of the area before the war and nightmares of wartime. He mentioned that a friend of his was kidnapped and killed in West Beirut. He indicated that he was not sure of his feelings toward the area in the aftermath of the war by saying, "I just don't go there! I am not used to it!" He shrugged and added, "Anyway, I have no reason to be there!"

However, while the once-prohibited East and West Beirut had become relatively accessible, in the immediate aftermath of the war, a new area, the downtown, had been deemed off-limits for all city residents after it was turned into a construction site for international investment. Subsequently, this prohibited space became a symbolic space—a site of nostalgia—that people could only access through remembrance. For example, when Solidere demolished the prewar markets of Beirut, many people started to revalue their personal and collective memories about these lost sites. Nostalgia about prewar and wartime spaces and experiences was a way of expressing feelings of loss, exclusion, and helplessness in the present.

While the powerless groups and individuals were excluded from the

A bombed-out building near the Green Line

process of reconstruction, investors, developers, and governmental institutions that controlled the physical rebuilding of the city were shaping Beirut's past and history through the deployment of new meanings assigned to selected urban spaces. They started designating buildings and spaces as historically valuable landmarks, erecting monuments, while removing or relocating other national symbols based on specific interpretations of the past that suited their momentary interests.

Discourses of the past are cultural reconstructions of time and space (Alonso 1994; Berliner 2005; Boyarin 1994). Christopher Tilley (1994) asserts that spatial experiences and memories are not neutral, but connected to social relationships and positions of power. Following Tilley's assertion, I suggest that "ordinary practitioners of the city" rely on their past experiences and memories of selected urban spaces to secure a role in determining the future of their own city. In Beirut, hegemonic groups (urban planners and developers, backed by politicians) attempted to accommodate and even appropriate the voices of the less powerful by recurrently reshaping their discourses on urban planning and design and announcing plans to "protect the heritage" by preserving selected urban sites or monuments. The competition over appropriation, use, and preservation of urban spaces between the dominant actors and the "ordinary practitioners of the city" leaves us with the following questions: How do memory and remembrance affect the power relationships embedded and manifested in the complex process of negotiation over space? How do disenfranchised groups strategically use and manipulate space to evade attempts by the powerful to "discipline" them and regulate their spatial relationships and activities?

CHANGING METHODOLOGIES AND IDENTITIES

As the physical landscapes changed constantly, Beirutis lived in a state of liminality and uncertainty. Therefore, conducting fieldwork in an unstable environment required flexible methodologies and techniques to accommodate the emerging needs. Traditional anthropologists have been criticized as they traveled to faraway places where they found "small and simple" communities, and avoided sites and communities characterized by complexity, literacy, historical depth, and structural messiness (Appadurai 1986). However, in the past two decades, anthropologists have documented the challenges they encountered while conducting research in conflict zones (Daniel 1996; Feldman 1995; Kovats-Bernat 2002; Sluka 2000). These writings questioned traditional anthropological methods and allowed researchers to reassess their relationship to the field and to their interlocutors. In what follows, I present the hindrances I faced in Lebanon and then discuss the methods and techniques I used to gather and analyze anthropological data in postwar Beirut.

It was a challenge to conduct anthropological research in an unpredictable, transitional, yet modern urban context. In fact, Beirut was a "nontraditional" fieldsite destination, and my relationship to this research project was neither that of the outsider anthropologist who studies the "other" nor that of the indigenous/native anthropologist who conducts research among "her own people."[5] When I began my research project in Beirut, I faced a number of challenges, both because of the dramatic changes in the postwar city and because of my "politically problematic identity." It was difficult to keep track of the constant changes in the urban landscape. At first, neighborhoods disappeared, buildings were dynamited while many others were constructed, and major new highways were paved while smaller roads were blocked. Moreover, the whole downtown area was demolished to make way for the future modern city center. I found that these transformations in the urban environment distorted the social relationships among the residents of the city and their relations to their once-familiar city spaces. Just as residents of many other urban centers, Beirutis were forced to employ multiple strategies in their daily lives to survive the difficulties they encountered. They proclaimed multiple identities, formed formal and informal alliances, and established socioeconomic and political networks to negotiate for urban rights and services.

Like the residents of the city, as a researcher, I had to alter my politically complex identity to cope with this challenging urban setting. During my stay in Beirut, I was forced to adopt some identities and renounce others as needed. On several occasions, I described myself and my interlocutors described me along real and—sometimes—invented identities, including nationality, university affiliation (American University of Beirut, AUB; and City University of New York), profession, and marital status. Whatever identity I assumed, it affected whom I could interview and what information my interlocutors would share with me. The necessity of adopting multiple identities raised serious questions regarding power relations when conducting field research and ethical questions regarding the relationship between anthropologists and their subjects.

On my first exploratory visit to Beirut, in June 1995, I assumed that as an Arab woman, I would be studying an area culturally and socially similar to my own. I spoke the same language, grew up and lived in neighboring countries, and thus assumed that Lebanon, its people, practices, and cultures would be familiar and accessible to my anthropological endeavor.

Unfortunately, upon my arrival in Beirut, I realized that I had been wrong. First, I was disappointed when I found that being a Palestinian and non-Lebanese was in fact a limiting factor. Palestinians in Lebanon were looked down upon because it was generally assumed that they live in refugee camps in a state of extreme poverty. A number of my informants were surprised to know that not all Palestinians lived in refugee camps.[6] This placed me outside stereotypical Lebanese social frameworks and put me in a category of a Palestinian who is not a refugee. During conversations about my background, my Arabic dialect, and my research interests, interlocutors sometimes stated, "Look, she is so friendly, as if she were not a Palestinian." This comment was meant as a compliment and a sign that the speakers had accepted me.

When I sensed my Palestinian identity might cause problems, I introduced myself to some of my interlocutors as a "researcher from Jordan" (after all, I carried a Jordanian passport during my fieldwork). In some instances, being a Jordanian and not a Palestinian created an assumed alliance between us. Some even expressed their acceptance of me by stating "we both suffered from the presence of Palestinians in our countries." Conducting fieldwork immediately after the war was an additional challenge, since Palestinians had taken part in it and were viewed by many Lebanese as troublemakers and outsiders. Furthermore, Palestinians were also blamed for bringing their battles to the shores of Lebanon. Even those Lebanese who were sympathetic to the Palestinian plight questioned my commitment to my own people and were skeptical about my research interests. They advised me to go to the refugee camps and investigate the terrible conditions so that my research might ease the misery (*ta'teer*) of "my people." Interestingly, I found that Western (French, German, Swedish, and American) researchers working in Beirut were not questioned about their choice of subject or about the application of their research to implement social and political changes.

However, despite these questions about my national identity, the fact that I was an Arab, in many instances, gave me the status of a local researcher. This shared background allowed me to engage in intellectual discussions with Lebanese scholars on such topics as the objectivity of researchers who work with their "own people," the role of social scientists in helping to implement social and political change, the differences between the responsibilities of local/indigenous versus outsider/Western researchers, and the role of the local intelligentsia in the Arab world.

For instance, when I spoke to a Lebanese social scientist, he differentiated between the role of Western and Arab researchers. He argued that Western researchers, even those who are sensitive to local customs and causes, when they finish their projects, can shrug and say "too bad you have all of these problems, I am done with my research, good luck and good-bye." He felt that Arab researchers do not have the same choice.

They cannot leave these problems behind. Either they stay, or they invest themselves in these causes and work to find solutions even after they finish their research. "I know there are no direct solutions for most of the problems in our boiling region," he added; "this is why we get frustrated, our 'blood boils' and many of us die of heart attacks."

Additionally, my Arab identity allowed me to socialize and work with faculty in the social sciences and humanities at the Lebanese University and the American University of Beirut and with local activists and intellectuals. Toward the end of my stay in Beirut, I gave talks about the relationship between anthropology and colonialism, discussed my research with graduate students, and lectured on the differences in higher education in the United States and Arab countries.[7] This environment allowed me to take part in informal and intimate discussions about the history and identity of Beirut. Such encounters enriched the data I gathered regarding the discourses about the reconstruction project and made the concerns of local intellectuals an inevitable part of this ethnography.

Another identity that paved the way to a whole set of research possibilities was that of a researcher from New York. This facilitated affiliations with the American University of Beirut (AUB) and the French Centre d'Etudes et de Recherches sur le Moyen-Orient Contemporain (CERMOC). Both institutions allowed me access to research libraries, special collections, and archives as well as the chance to interact closely with other scholars. My affiliation with AUB made conducting interviews with locals, especially those who lived in the vicinity of the university, possible. In fact, many Beirutis were accustomed to AUB students and researchers carrying out research projects. My affiliation with a university in New York helped to schedule appointments with journalists, politicians, and officials at governmental institutions. For example, when I was invited to present my research project to a graduate anthropology class at the Lebanese University, the professor introduced me by saying, "She is coming all the way from New York to study 'Ayn el-Mreisse—just one neighborhood! This is how Americans do anthropology." In this context, I was viewed as an American anthropologist.

Just as with the experiences noted in the writings by other Arab female anthropologists who conducted fieldwork among Middle Eastern communities, my gender identity shaped the data I gathered.[8] In the anthology *Arab Women in the Field*, Altorki and El-Solh (1988) suggest that the status of a female ethnographer is both more empowering and more confining than the status of Arab male ethnographers. For example, despite an awareness of her complex position as an insider and an outsider,

Suad Joseph (1988) found in her research that it was necessary for her to behave like a "proper Lebanese woman" to gain the trust of the community she studied in the neighborhood of Borj Ḥammoud. My own identity as an Arab woman, I found, played a major role in shaping the data I gathered. The fact that I was an Arab woman allowed me access to the domestic world of women; however, I had to meet the "modesty" expectations of my interlocutors. For example, three days after I rented a furnished apartment in ʿAyn el-Mreisse, where many displaced families and prostitutes lived, my next-door neighbor brought her hookah and came to have coffee with me but also to find out more about my personal life. Her first comment was: "I did not see you hanging any laundry on your balcony. I guess you do not have children—I hope God will give you some soon." My neighbor's statement implied a number of questions for which I felt obliged to provide answers. When she learned that I was single and did not, in fact, have children, she asked to use my balcony for her own laundry. She also subtly wanted to find out, on behalf of other neighbors, if I was a prostitute, as it was assumed that a single woman who rented furnished apartments in that neighborhood had to be. By observing my daily schedule and my clothes, it did not take my neighbors long to determine that I was not in that line of work. Later on, another neighbor told me: "Before letting you into our homes [for interviews and social visits] we watched you. You did not stand on the street corner after sunset to pick up customers, you did not receive single men in your apartment, and above all you dressed differently, and you wore eyeglasses. We knew you were not the usual kind of single woman who rents a furnished apartment." Even though I did not fit their stereotypes, nonetheless I became an object of their gazes, observations, and gossip.

In the course of gathering my data, my interviewees cast me in a particular mold according to their preconceived expectations. These projections filtered the kind of information and interpretations I gathered and shaped the outcome of the research project. For example, many of the people I interviewed found it curious that I inquired about their daily routines. Some remarked that such questions were usually asked by foreign researchers (*ajanib*), meaning Westerners, inferring that I should know these facts. This forced me to explain the scope of my study of "anthropology." One of my neighbors explained my purpose to others by saying, "She collects stories about old-time Beirut (Beirut *zaman*)"; "She is writing a book about the history of our neighborhood"; or, "She is writing a history of the original people of Beirut."

However, at the end of my stay in Beirut, my identity as an Arab, a Palestinian, a woman, and an anthropologist was challenged. After leaving for a three-day conference in Cairo, I was prevented by the Lebanese airport authorities from reentering Beirut. My affiliations with a number of research institutions and "connections" with "influential" individuals in Beirut could not override my "politically problematic identity" as a Palestinian, that is, a refugee. In fact, my Palestinian identity precluded permission to reenter my fieldsite, even for seventy-two hours in order to retrieve my field notes. Upon my return to New York without field notes, I had to rely on my memories to write about the way Beirutis remembered their own city and talked about their past experiences. Three months after leaving Beirut, I was fortunate that a Lebanese friend visited his family and brought most of the research data back to New York.

In addition to the obstacles I faced as a result of my multiple identities, there were other practical obstacles in researching a postwar urban environment. For example, accessing official and published materials necessary for the research was an elaborate task. During the war, many of the official records such as reports, maps, and city plans had been burned, lost, damaged, or moved to unknown locations, so it was almost impossible to locate or access documents and government reports. The few state agencies that had continued to function were relocated to "relatively safer areas," and some of them were divided across two or more offices because of the way the city was divided. For instance, the Municipality, located in the downtown area before the war, had to be divided and relocated on respective sides of the Green Line, in West and East Beirut.

The overlap in the responsibilities of the private sector and the different governmental and nongovernmental agencies also added to the challenge of locating postwar records. Moreover, because of the fragile sectarian environment of Lebanon, statistics and census materials were highly politicized documents. The first and only Lebanese national census was mandated by the French in 1932. According to this census, Lebanon was the only country in the region with a Christian majority (51 percent). Based on this census, significant government posts were divided proportionally among Lebanon's eighteen ethnoreligious groups: the president of the country was to be a Maronite Christian; the prime minister, a Sunni Muslim; and the speaker of the house, a Shi'ite Muslim. This system of representation was to be applied to all governmental posts respectively. Since then, every attempt to conduct a new census has been resisted. Sectarian groups have provided conflicting numbers for the size of each group, and these estimates have always been questioned and falsified by political rivals. Therefore, at the time of my fieldwork, it was almost impossible to rely on statistical data that varied from one source to another.[9]

Also, although as an Arab I could readily understand Arabic and nuances of the language, I still needed to acclimate to some local modes of speaking. Initially, I found it difficult to understand the sardonic tones of my interlocutors, especially when referring to the rebuilding of the city. For example, upon my arrival in Beirut, I was astonished at the responses to my inquiries about Solidere's role in the rebuilding of the downtown area, which provoked political jokes or sarcastic comments that dismissed the project as one big conspiracy (*mu'amara kabira*) or as nonsense (*tajleet*), without necessarily providing details. I heard locals use different names for the downtown area. During the early phases of the reconstruction project, they continued to use the area's prewar and wartime names of *al-balad*[10] or *wasaṭ al-balad*, names that had been used when the area housed the main markets, businesses, and entertainment activities and later the battlefields of the fighting militia. However, within a few months, when Beirutis realized that the city center would never return to what it had once been, they started to call it a-Solidere or "the ruins down there" (*al-atharat yalli taḥt*).[11]

Ethnography of postwar contexts requires anthropologists to invent and combine techniques in order to integrate various types of data and to fit sites that are in flux during the fieldwork itself into a larger anthropological interpretive framework. Moreover, urban ethnography often aims to juxtapose multiple perspectives on the same location. For this reason, this ethnography does not document a single urban neighborhood or specific ethnic group, but rather the transformations of multiple urban spaces and the ways they were used, remembered, and narrated. My core data consist of formal and informal interviews with a range of individuals and groups I described above. These one-on-one interactions with a diverse array of speakers allowed me to represent multiple worlds, from the unemployed to laborers to middle-class professionals, from illegal to legal tenants and their landlords, from arts to religion to business, which I hope creates a multiple-perspective vision of the postwar cityscape. Given the importance of printed writings, I made considerable use of "hegemonic texts," or printed voices of the empowered (memoirs by residents of the city; newspaper articles written by historians, architects, archaeologists, and journalists; official and nonofficial reports from government agencies, development firms, and political parties; and conference papers).

Through this combination of voices and techniques, this ethnography records a transitional betwixt-and-between moment in Beirut's history. It documents a period when Beirutis had to put their lives on hold while the future of their city was shaped by the interests of regional and global developers in ways they could not have predicted prior to the war.

This chapter discusses the discourses surrounding Solidere's reconstruction project in Beirut's Central District (BCD). After a brief description of Solidere's plans to reconstruct the downtown area, I present the responses of two groups who were excluded from participating in defining the future of the city. The first group consisted of intellectuals, historians, architects, and social scientists who voiced their opposition to Solidere's plans through publishing "hegemonic texts" and holding meetings. The second group consisted of less powerful collectives such as the displaced families, local residents, and long-standing tenants who defied Solidere's plans. They voiced their opposition by evoking their prewar and wartime spatial memories, announcing religious decrees (*fatwa*s), spreading rumors in informal gatherings, and forming neighborhood collectives. Both groups took it upon themselves to preserve the city's endangered past and the heritage of its diverse ethnic groups. They doubted Solidere's promotional motto "Beirut an Ancient City of the Future."

In analyzing the debates among intellectuals, political and religious leaders, property owners, and the population displaced by the war, the following questions must be addressed: In whose image and to whose benefit is space shaped and reconstructed? How is space influenced by powers of domination (Harvey 1989, 177–178)? How does the inclusion and exclusion of spatial memories take place? Which sites and locations are to be preserved for the future? And for whom? To answer these questions, I discuss how certain binary concepts such as public/private, traditional/modern, hegemonic/powerless, and remembering/forgetting are constructed and questioned through the representations and interpretations of space/place and time/history.

AN ABSENT STATE

During the sixteen-year Lebanese civil war (1975–1991), the state and its agencies were completely absent. Government institutions failed to provide the services they had supplied before the war after militias and political parties took over the army, the municipalities, and television and radio stations, and after soldiers and policemen deserted their positions and joined militias based on their sectarian affiliation.[1] This absence of a single, unifying political power left a void later filled by Prime Minister Rafik Hariri.[2]

By the late 1970s, five years after the beginning of the war, militias and ideological groups had become highly effective politico-military machines. They developed sophisticated bureaucracies and provided public services, collected ransoms, ran educational institutions, provided health services, controlled markets and ports, operated radio and television stations, and published newspapers (Denoeux 1993, 92). Accordingly, residents of Beirut found themselves interacting with militiamen and other armed groups on a daily basis. Militiamen acted as mediators when conflict erupted between neighbors, they housed the war-displaced, and they offered jobs for the unemployed. Merchants and shop owners solicited militia members to protect them and their properties and in return paid protection money; owners of residential buildings maintained a subordinate relation with militias in charge of their neighborhoods by offering them vacant apartments; and the children of the displaced families joined these militias as fighters. The majority of the interlocutors I interviewed in Beirut recalled occasions when they solicited the help of militias in securing food, shelter, security, employment, water, or electricity. Under these circumstances, sectarian or confessional identity had become a viable medium for survival. "Without it [confessional identity], one was, literally, rootless, nameless, and voiceless. . . . One was not heard or recognized unless one's confessional allegiance was disclosed first. It was only when one was placed within a confessional context that one's ideas and assertions were rendered meaningful or worthwhile" (Khalaf and Denoeux 1988, 192, 196).

The devastating sixteen-year civil war formally ended in 1991 after most of the combating parties signed the Taif Accord. Accordingly, a new government was formed by Prime Minister Rafik Hariri; the country's constitution was revised, giving more power to underrepresented confessional groups; and most of the militias were disarmed. Although the war ended, postwar government institutions continued to be subjected to the interference of political parties, warlords, and traditional leadership, in addition to regional and international developers. The challenges confronting the Hariri government were to restore the authority of the state, to reunify the army and the police forces, and to rehabilitate the damaged infrastructure. Moreover, the government needed to reconcile the conflicting groups, solve the problem of thousands of displaced families, rebuild the war-torn city, and, most importantly, secure enough financial resources to carry out all of these projects.

Prime Minister Hariri relied heavily on the private sector to carry out many of the postwar projects. For example, Solidere was the only private company he charged with rebuilding Beirut's Central District. After narrating Solidere's public relations tour of the downtown, I recount its plans, along with the debates, criticism, and opposition those raised among empowered voices (I turn to other voices in subsequent chapters), with reference to theories of space and memory.

TOURING THE DOWNTOWN AREA

In an effort to introduce its plans and to familiarize investors, tourists, and city residents with its vision of the future downtown area, Solidere organized public events in the destroyed downtown area. Among these events were free tours conducted in English and French. In October 1996, I participated in an English-language tour. The participants met the guide in front of Solidere's offices, in the heart of the destroyed Central District. The tour began with a visit to a large air-conditioned white tent nearby to view an architectural model of the area. Using a laser pointer, the guide showed the group the model's miniature streets, governmental offices, residential areas, and sites of worship. In a misguided effort by Solidere to demonstrate environmental sensibility, the sightseers were then driven by bus through the empty construction site, making a stop at the recycling project. Then we were brought to a site where archaeologists were unearthing artifacts later to be documented and relocated to an archaeological park.[3] Afterward, the participants were guided to vacant houses of worship, mosques and churches. For safety, the visitors were given hard hats marked with the company's logo before they entered a church under restoration. Finally, the two-hour tour ended with a lecture by a high-ranking employee at Solidere's headquarters. The lecturer explained the economic aspects of the reconstruction project and the fluctuation in the financial market in an effort to sell shares.

Solidere's architectural model of downtown Beirut, displayed at the visitors' tent

SOLIDERE: PLANS TO REBUILD DOWNTOWN BEIRUT

Despite heated discussions and disputes concerning the details of the reconstruction plan, there was a consensus among the Lebanese public regarding the need to rebuild Beirut's city center for economic and social reasons. Economically, it was believed that rebuilding the Central District would allow Beirut to reclaim its prewar role as the financial capital of the Middle East. Socially, the downtown area represented a site of national harmony among the combating groups. Prior to the war, it was the place where different classes, religious sects, and ideologies interacted, thus the revitalization of this area was presented as a way to heal the wounds of the war. Sociologist Samir Khalaf describes the prewar city center as a peaceful site for the mingling of heterogeneous elements: rural/urban, Christian/Muslim, Lebanese/Palestinian, Sunni/Shi'ite, religious/secular, rich/poor, and local/international. For Khalaf, the rebuilding of Beirut's Central District was intended to create a city where previously warring factions would live and interact in relative harmony in what he named the future "melting pot" (Khalaf 1994, 2006).

In 1992, the first postwar government formed by the billionaire prime minister Rafik Hariri introduced a grand plan to rebuild downtown Beirut. To ease the financial burden, the newly formed government granted private regional and international investors a major role in the rebuilding initiatives. The government adopted a long-term plan called Horizon 2000 to completely privatize Beirut's Central District. This plan would allow regional and foreign capital—in the form of loans and grants from the European Union, the World Bank, UN agencies, and Arab countries—to finance the large-scale reconstruction project. Before he became prime minister of Lebanon, Rafik Hariri had worked in real estate and owned a number of construction companies in Saudi Arabia. In Lebanon, he continued to invest in real estate and construction. It was rumored that he was the largest property owner in Lebanon, and he also owned a newspaper and a television station.

The privatization of downtown Beirut reached its height in May 1994 when the Hariri government appointed the private joint-stock company Solidere to finance, restore, and oversee the reconstruction and rehabilitation of Beirut's Central District. Opponents criticized Solidere for overlooking the needs of the residents of Beirut and destroying the city's rich heritage. It was rumored that Hariri himself owned more than 50 percent of the company's shares. Journalist Vanessa Martin described Solidere as "Hariri's profit-making puppet" and criticized it for ignoring the city's rich past by attempting "to build Manhattan-style skyscrapers" (1997, 763).

Solidere presented its plans as the largest worldwide urban redevelopment project of the 1990s. It proposed to create a central district that would compete with other eastern Mediterranean city centers, and that would attract regional and foreign investments. Mobilizing the attachment of many Lebanese to prewar Beirut, Solidere portrayed its plans as part of a larger endeavor for the city to reclaim its prewar financial and regional role. In *Beirut Reborn* (a coffee-table book published by Solidere), Angus Gavin and Ramez Maluf (1996, 36) nostalgically described prewar Beirut as a place where

> an international community felt very much at home [and] a mixed community of 40,000 lived there. Prewar Beirut was a microcosm of Lebanon's multifaceted society. It was preeminent in banking, financial services, insurance, maritime agencies and other commercial office and trading functions that serviced both the region and the whole Arab world.

In addition to stressing the city's prewar economic role, Solidere brought into play the nationalist role of its project. One of the company's senior architects stated that Solidere's "massive reconstruction of down-town Beirut was seen as a must-do action to announce the end of war and the beginning of the return to normality" (Kabbani 1996, 8). Another Solidere representative suggested the plan would re-create the "micro-cosm" of Lebanon and that for Beirut to regain its prewar role, "she"[4] should revive its downtown area.

> The character of the prewar city center and the special nature of the place—its history, association with sea and mountains, economic role in the region, and links with east and west—are real assets. These will be brought to life once again through the reconstruction of the Central District. (Gavin and Maluf 1996, 12–13)

Hariri effectively suppressed some ideas of national history and ex-ploited others in order to launch a new nationalist unifying project. Soli-dere as well as its opponents all agreed that the city's past and identity should be preserved. The questions left unanswered were: What kinds of previous roles should the future Beirut maintain? and Who had the authority to define the city's contested pasts and identities?

Solidere's reconstruction project encompassed the BCD area, once the main commercial district, and the city center. The project covered 1.8 million square meters, including 608,000 square meters of reclaimed land on the sea front. The built-up area was intended to include offices, commercial centers, residential buildings, government offices, worship places, cultural facilities, and hotels. The remaining area consisting of roads, utilities, and public gardens would be declared government prop-erties (Solutions Group [SARL] 1997, 47).

Solidere's capital consisted of the shares of property right holders, owners, and tenants and stock market shares. According to the plan, pre-war owners and tenants whose property was confiscated by Solidere were to be allocated 50 percent of the company's total shares based on the esti-mated value of their property. The other half, however, was earmarked for outside investors (Beyhum et al. 1992).

Solidere's plans provoked vigorous debates concerning the future and the past of Beirut. Participants in this discourse included funding agen-cies that had different techno-economic interests; urban planners and ar-chitects whose main concern was the aesthetics and physical appearance of the future city; Lebanese social scientists, historians, and writers who championed the call to preserve the city's cultural heritage and past; tra-ditional local, religious, and political leaders whose concern was to maintain their power, influence, and followers; prewar users of the space, such as tenants and property owners; displaced groups who occupied different spaces in the city during and after the war; and semigovernmental institutions like the Awqaf, the organization that managed religiously endowed properties.

INVOKING MEMORIES OF THE PAST

Although Solidere expressed interest in preserving Beirut's heritage in its promotional literature, opponents criticized its plans for considering only physical appearance and future revenue and for ignoring the social aspects of reconstruction, public interests and needs, residents' diverse historical pasts, and their memories of intimate urban places (Al-Abdulah 1993; Beyhum 1996; Beyhum et al. 1992; Corm 1994; Dajani 1994; Davey 2000; Dnawi 1994; Khalaf 1993; Khalaf and Khoury 1993; Khoury 1995; Labaki 1993; Najem 2000; Seeden 1993). The critics believed the plan was designed as though the old center had never existed, even though "people have not yet forgotten the city center . . . [; they] are attached emotionally to their previous places" (Nasr 1993, 65).

While the reconstruction company destroyed what remained of the city center, dynamiting the buildings and bulldozing the streets, Beirut residents (both powerful and powerless) expressed sorrow at seeing the downtown area disappearing and many of the city's landmarks being demolished. This massive destruction provoked many Beirutis to document their personal prewar and wartime experiences and to express their pain about the damage caused by bulldozers. One writer recalled his childhood memories of walking happily in the old downtown area: "[I remember] the alleys where we used to wander around as children, the *kunafa* [a traditional Arabic dessert] places, the small shops with colored glass, the Martyrs' Square, and the streets that were crowded with pedestrians." The author shifts to the present time to depict with sorrow what he witnessed after a recent visit to the same area:

> Yesterday we visited a ghost town that lay in the midst of the dust of its destroyed buildings and engulfed by the noise of big construction equipment. The photographers pointed their cameras, waiting to document the minute of destroying the Rivoli [a prewar movie theater]. . . . Minutes later, the Rivoli shined with a huge light and the dust covered the whole area. At that moment the sign of the "Orient"[5] that survived

the war years collapsed on top of the body of the dead building. This pile of rubble buried beneath it our childhood cries and the dreams of many Beirutis. (*Al-Safir,* April 6, 1994)

The helplessness and inability of the city dwellers to stop Solidere's calculated destruction was vividly illustrated through a description of the photographers' hands that held the cameras waiting to document the death of one of the city's major landmarks. City residents were incapable of protecting one of their childhood sites, but they insisted on witnessing, documenting, and mourning its destruction. The publication of these nostalgic accounts in daily newspapers allowed personal narratives to enter the public sphere and transformed private memories into acts of collective remembering.

Writers deemed Solidere responsible for the dismantling of Beirut's past and for the erasure of its residents' memories. Elias Khoury, a Lebanese novelist and journalist, warned the public that Beirut was destroying itself and that it would suffer a frightening amnesia. He described the city center as "an empty space, a placeless space, and a hole in the memory" (1995). He alerted his fellow residents to the dangers of the fearsome amnesia. According to Khoury, destroying Beirut's history and forgetting its past were represented in empty and hollow spaces in what was left of the downtown area.

Khoury attributed his sense of loss and helplessness to Solidere's power and authority to shatter people's memories of the downtown area. Feeling that everyday life no longer had its "taken-for-grantedness," Lebanese writers like Khoury invoked the past by recalling specific landscapes, monuments, landmarks, and detailed spatial experiences. This process of remembering was a cry for recognition and a protest against the exclusion from deciding the future of their city.

Solidere's failure to consider prewar and wartime experiences and spaces became a major concern for Lebanese intellectuals. Archaeologists, historians, architects, urban planners, and social scientists all expressed the common concern that Solidere's plan was designed as if the area had no history, and its residents had no emotional and spatial attachment to its urban spaces. These specialists urged Solidere to preserve historically valuable buildings and sites that represent Beirut's threatened past and heritage. Suzy Hakimian, a Lebanese archaeologist, underscored the importance of cooperation between architects, archaeologists, and city planners and emphasized that archaeological and historical preservation should not be an obstacle to the reconstruction project (1994, 17).

Others advocated the preservation of designated buildings and monuments. Jad Tabet, a Lebanese architect, recommended preserving historical sites that might enhance the city's future by allowing the past and the future to intertwine. The historically imbued spaces and symbols would consider new ideas and activities. Tabet warned of implementing the "Tabula Rasa"[6] architectural method, as had been done when rebuilding the war-destroyed cities of The Hague, Tokyo, and Berlin. Tabet recommended the restoration method, where city centers were rehabilitated, as in Bologna, West Berlin, Lisbon, and Mexico City (Tabet 1994, 79).

A CONTESTED PAST: CONFLICTING NARRATIVES OF DESTRUCTION AND CONSTRUCTION

In the aftermath of the war, Beirut's five thousand years of history became a contested domain among its eighteen multi-ethnoreligious communities. These ethnic and religious groups invoked the past and claimed roots in the city. Authors wrote historical accounts in which they underscored certain aspects of the past and suppressed others. I argue that these contradictory interpretations of the past emerged as a response to the uncertain conditions of the present and an unpredictable future. For example, some historians who accused Solidere of destroying the present city assured their readers that Beirut had been destroyed many times by wars, natural disasters, and corrupt leadership, and yet its loyal residents were able to rebuild it (Jarkas 1996; Tirawi 2004).

On the other hand, historians who supported Hariri and Solidere evoked Beirut's ancient past as a prominent Phoenician port that offered refuge to "strangers," who then obliterated the city when they fomented trouble by making its leaders wage wars against each other. These narratives blamed the "outsiders" for the destruction of Beirut but offered hope by assuring their readers that the faithful "sons" of the city, who remained steadfast, were able to protect their city.[7] These historians suggest that Beirut was destroyed during the civil war when its treacherous citizens collaborated with the outsiders (*ghuraba'a*). Even though Hariri was an "outsider"[8] to many Beirutis, they trusted that Solidere would save the city. For example, a Beiruti historian unearthed a story that was first recorded in 1926 and rewrote the following account in the mid-1990s:

In 147 BC, Eskandar Balla took over Beirut and claimed himself its king. A vigorous war took place between Balla [the illegitimate outsider] and the city's legal king, Dimitryous II. Beirut honorably defended its legitimate king, who won the war. Later on, Balla's minister, Tryphon Eskandar, betrayed the king when he collaborated with Dimitryous, son of Antokhous VI, and attacked Beirut, destroyed its buildings, and burned it down. It is believed that Beirut remained a destroyed city for the following one hundred years. (Cheikho 1993 [1926], 32)

To understand the significance of this historical account in the context of postwar Beirut, we need to look at the postwar discourses surrounding Solidere's rebuilding project. These narratives posited that the "unfaithful sons" or the illegitimate outsiders are the Lebanese militia who destroyed the city on behalf of foreign powers. However, the rebuilding of the city, according to the postwar narratives in support of Solidere, was carried out by a new symbolic king, Prime Minister Rafik Hariri.

Yet other historians[9] relied on fatalistic explanations for the destruction of the Phoenician city. They cite stories in which the gods sent earthquakes and fires to punish the disloyal corrupt residents who did not appreciate their gift of a prosperous town. For example, in his recent memoir *Oh, for Those Old Days, Beirut*, the *mukhtar*[10] of the Ras Beirut area, Kamal Jurji Rbeiz, writes that "the oldest city in the world . . . the most ancient Phoenician city" had been destroyed several times by the gods because of the actions of its residents. He described the city's glorious past by enumerating a series of events that took place there. In 64 BC, it was a large, prosperous Roman center of culture, the arts, and theater. Later, in the third century, it became the site of a major Roman law school. But in 349, 494, 502, and 551, a series of earthquakes destroyed a large part of the city. Because of these earthquakes, the sea penetrated a mile inland and shattered what was left of the city. A few years later, it was rebuilt yet again, but in 610 the new buildings were completely destroyed by fire (Rbeiz 1986, 13). A survivor had the destroyed Beirut speak these words:

> I am the most pessimistic city and the least lucky. . . . I saw the dead bodies of my sons in the fields when the god of fire attacked me with hot burning arrows. Today the god of the sea flooded me with its angry waves. Where is my glorious beauty? My glorious days were taken away. I became mere rubble. . . . Oh passersby, cry for my bad luck and cry for me, the shrinking Beirut. (Rbeiz 1986, 15)

Although Beirut's Phoenician past was emphasized, other moments of the city's history were written about, even though they received less attention. For example, a few authors wrote about the Arab Muslim conquest in the seventh century and the invasion of the Crusaders at the end of the eleventh century. More frequently, historians, architects, and geographers resurrected the city's Ottoman and French colonial past and debated the comparative merits of the urban plans drawn up by these two powers. Early Ottoman Beirut was a small walled town surrounded by gardens until it was named a "Turkish vilayet" in 1840; then in 1876, it expanded over the neighboring hills after the Ottomans had demolished its medieval wall (Murno 1987).

The Ottoman plan was grand, designed to revitalize the downtown area to house major government buildings. However, Assem Salam, a Lebanese architect, rejected the Ottoman plans because they demolished large areas of the medieval city and flattened many of its commercial and residential areas in order to build wide avenues and monumental government buildings (1998, 122–123). Michael Davie, a geographer and urban historian, instead endorsed the same Ottoman plans and viewed them as a form of "positive controlled urbanization" accompanied by organic aesthetic norms and infrastructure that the local population helped shape. Davie credited the Ottomans' contribution in establishing public gardens, schools, and hospitals. In fact, Davie reminds us that the Ottomans provided Beirut "with an Islamic identity by building the three-arched, red-tiled roof family house" (1998, 3).[11]

The construction of this Ottoman city[12] came to a halt because of the outbreak of World War I and the subsequent bombing of Beirut by the Italians. Despite the destruction, much of the Ottoman monumental architecture had survived and some continues to exist to this day. For example, the Grand Sarai building that once housed the Ottoman government was renovated by Solidere to temporarily function as the headquarters of its Council for Development and Reconstruction and later to house the office of the prime minister.

Lebanon was ruled by the French immediately after World War I. At that point, the French took it upon themselves to draw up a new design for the city of Beirut. They introduced French-style buildings and changed the architectural fabric of the city. Western-style architecture replaced the old, especially when many affluent Beirutis adopted this new French architectural style. Boulevards and public squares were now given names such as Clemenceau, Foch, Place de l'Etoile, and Place de l'Opera.

Some scholars viewed these French plans as a constructive effort to organize the city, but others saw them as a form of colonial domination that destroyed the Arab-Islamic identity of the city. Assem Salam viewed these new plans as salvation from the Ottoman destruction of the city's medieval past. He justified these plans by saying, "[The French] found an old city partly demolished, and immediately developed an ambitious scheme for its improvement. New axial roads were established and named after French and other European celebrities, and a renovation [plan for] the city center [was drafted]" (Salam 1998, 122–123). Davie, on the other hand, considered the French to be colonizers who left a negative imprint on the city. He argued that when the French took over in 1919, Beirut already had a vibrant business center, with distinct architecture and a coherent urban plan. "The French military authorities planned the capital almost as if it was a North African colony. Their first action was to surround it with barracks, then to link the port to these defensive points. The second action was to destroy the heart of the city and reorganize the road system, mirroring the Place de l'Etoile in Paris" (Davie 1998, 3).

In 1943, a national government replaced French rule, and Lebanon became an independent state. Many Lebanese described the period between the inception of independence and 1975, when the civil war broke out, as "the golden days." During this time, Lebanon was called the "Switzerland of the East," and its capital, Beirut, the "Paris of the Arab World," the "Jewel of the Orient," and the "East's window onto the West." Despite its limited material resources, Beirut prospered economically due primarily to its "open market economy" amid the political turmoil that plagued the surrounding countries. The influx of oil revenue from the Gulf region, the vast amounts of money brought in by Syrian and Egyptian bourgeoisie after the nationalization of their economies, and the investments of Palestinians after the Israeli occupation of their country all contributed to Beirut becoming the financial capital of the region. However, this sudden economic prosperity was coupled with a steady stream of poor immigrants from the rural areas that fundamentally reshaped the urban landscape.

This influx of newcomers created an urgent need for housing, urban services, and infrastructure. Shiber[13] describes the new landscape as an "urban chaos," where "the downtown area was over-built by the addition of supplementary floors on top of the existing buildings and in the in-filling of all open spaces, . . . [new buildings] spread along the main arteries, swallowing up the beaches and crawling up the scenic mountain slopes" (cited in Tabet 1993, 85). Many of the new immigrants lived as squatters on the outskirts of the city and created what came to be known as the Misery Belt (Ḥizam al-Bou's) (Shararah 1985).[14]

In an effort to reduce this urban chaos, in 1952, the Camille Chamoun government presented its first master plan for Beirut.[15] Interestingly, it was a revised version of an earlier French plan drafted by the celebrated colonial architect Michel Ecochard in 1943. Just as with the Ottoman and French plans, this one was only partially completed. The only phases of the plan to be carried out were the demolition of many of the old structures and the paving of new streets to solve the problem of congested traffic (Salam 1970; Saliba 2000, 2004).[16]

Twenty years later, the civil war broke out and destroyed most of Beirut's Central District. In fact, the once-lively downtown area became a ghost town inhabited only by snipers, militias, and stray animals.[17] During periods of cease fire, the successive war governments launched yet other plans to revive downtown Beirut (Khalaf and Khoury 1993). Local residents also took part in the construction of the city. Property owners, tenants, and the displaced continuously repaired their war-shattered homes, added extra floors to accommodate displaced relatives, and continued to build in the relatively safer but ever-changing areas of the city (Sarkis 1993).

This wartime turmoil has been extensively documented by historians, novelists, and filmmakers. Although the war lasted for almost two decades, it was often portrayed as momentary and exceptional or, as Syrian novelist Ghada al-Samman called it in her novel, "a series of nightmares" (1997). Memoirs were written to express sentiments about endangered and lost sites and carried nostalgic titles such as *Beirut in the Heart* (Jarkas 1996); *Oh, for Those Old Days, Beirut* (Rbeiz 1986); *Beirut Fragments* (Makdisi 1990); *Memory for Forgetfulness* (Darwish 1995); *Nadia, Captive of Hope: Memoir of an Arab Woman* (Kanafani 1998); *A Wish That Will Never Come True: June–October 1982* (Traboulsi 1984); *Our Beirut* (Itani and Fakhouri 1996); *Beirut the Heritage* (Al-Khatib 1993); and *Beirut: Morning Beauty* (Machnouk 1994). Literary works described the wartime city as a ghost town (Khouri 1990), and in other cases it was personified as a woman, specifically as a prostitute available to strangers (Adonis 1985); a lonely, sad widow; or a mother who gave birth only to unfaithful children (Kabani 1988). Novelists and filmmakers proliferated and expressed the loss of intimate places filled with memory. They depicted the brutality of the war and condemned its participants by crafting malicious protagonists who blindly joined the militias and participated in the destruction. These novels include *Beirut Blues* (Shaykh 1995), *Beirut Nightmares* (Al-Samman 1997), *Leaving Beirut: Women and the Wars Within* (Ghoussoub 1998), *The Stone of Laughter* (Barakat 1995), *Dear Mr. Kawabata* (Al-Daif 1999), *De Niro's Game* (Hage 2006), and *Koolaids: The Art of War* (Alameddine

1998). Similarly, films such as *West Beirut: Coming of Age in a Time of War*, *Between Us Two . . . Beirut*, *The Civilized People*, and *In the Battlefield* all depicted the ruthless conflict.

These contradictory accounts of the past were produced at a crucial time when the physical structure changed dramatically and the downtown area, "the heart of Beirut," was about to be destroyed/rebuilt one more time.

SAVING "HISTORICALLY VALUABLE" SITES

Despite the general outcry to conserve Beirut's threatened heritage, there was no consensus about what aspects of the past had to be preserved and which parts had to be forgotten and destroyed. Activists and intellectuals compelled Solidere to designate a number of buildings and monuments as "historically valuable." Nonetheless, they did not actually define which buildings they wanted to salvage or for whom.

In response to the general demand of conserving the city's past, Solidere hired architects, archaeologists, and urban planners. Some of them were among those who had criticized the initial plans. The newly formed committee was given the task of singling out "historically valuable" buildings in the downtown area. Accordingly, 265 buildings and monuments were designated as historically valuable (Solutions Group [SARL] 1997, 48). For Solidere, these buildings were meant to be symbols of Beirut's architectural heritage that "imbue the new city center with symbolic and aesthetic references to the past" (Percy 1995; Director General of Antiquities of Lebanon 1995). Additionally, two neighborhoods, Al-Saifi, located east of the city center, and Wadi Abu Jmil to the west, were to be renovated to their "original" architectural style and to be used as future residential areas.

Solidere employed a new approach to deliver its plans to the public and presented itself as the protector of the city's past and the guarantor of its heritage. It adopted the slogan "Beirut, an Ancient City of the Future" (Bayrut Madina 'Ariqa lil Mustaqbal). When I interviewed Ousama Kabbani, the head of Solidere's Department of Planning, he explained to me that Solidere's intention was to build a modern city that would have continuity with its past. He believed that taking the city's past into account would open up opportunities for a better future. He claimed that "the renewed city would thus speak to future generations from its own memory" (Kabbani 1996, 18).

Yet, Solidere's new approach of incorporating the city's past into its

A typical old Beiruti building

plans did not satisfy all the opponents of the project. Detractors argued that the restoration of selected buildings, while a positive step, simply removed them from their social and historical context. One male artist I interviewed described the result by saying, "The buildings looked like small creatures in the midst of a jungle of concrete and glass. Solidere only preserved the outside shells of the buildings and emptied the inside from history." The exterior might look the same as it did before the war, the artist argued, but its function, its users, and its meaning had changed.

Solidere's opponents succeeded in exerting their influence on the city's future plans by producing what could be called "hegemonic texts," that is, written material printed by powerful groups and individuals. Indeed, experts had published books, pamphlets, brochures, and articles that promoted their views. Such texts pressured Solidere to modify its plans a number of times to accommodate some aspects of their point of view.

Unlike the previously described intellectuals' plans that ignored Beirut's past and heritage, ordinary citizens developed nontextual opposition strategies. Beirutis claimed spatial urban identities, proclaimed space attachment to specific urban sites, and issued religious decrees (*fatwas*)[18] against Solidere and the Lebanese government. The reconstruction project became a central theme of public speeches, demonstrations, gossip, and jokes.

Religious parties issued religious *fatwas* against Solidere, its employees, and its shareholders. I interviewed Sheikh Ahmed, a leader of a Sunni religious party known as the Islamic Group (Al-Jama'á Al-Islameyá), who was critical of Solidere. Sheikh Ahmed voiced suspicions about the restoration intention of both the government and Solidere. He viewed the project as a conspiracy against the residents of the city. For him, the project was aimed at exploiting the local poor to benefit the rich international investors. He told me:

> Solidere's only concern is to bulldoze buildings that survived two decades of war and to replace them with glass towers and sell them to non-Lebanese rich investors. Go to downtown Beirut, and see for yourself. Solidere has demolished the houses and all the old popular souqs and left us, the people of the city, with bitterness and grief.[19]

The leadership of the political party (Al-Jama'á Al-Islameyá) voiced its opposition of Solidere by issuing a religious decree (*fatwa*) that made it illegal to buy Solidere's shares or participate in its schemes. However, the majority of the followers of the Islamic Group were largely from the less affluent members of society, those who did not have the means to buy Solidere's shares or take part in its plans.

Unlike Sheikh Ahmed of Al-Jama'á Al-Islameyá, other city residents who found themselves marginalized resorted to gossip and political jokes. For example, Abu Sami, a prewar resident and a business owner in downtown Beirut, had lost his business and home. During the war, he relocated to the adjacent neighborhood of 'Ayn el-Mreisse and opened a small grocery store. When I spoke to him at his shop, he sardonically expressed his dissatisfaction and helplessness toward the reconstruction project by saying: "What can I do? They [Solidere officials and the Lebanese government] disturbed the lives of the dead and the living alike. They took over everything. Solidere and Hariri dug out the bones of my father and mother and tossed them out into the sea. For the next Eid [a major Muslim holiday] I will go and pay my respects to my dead mother by visiting one of the Hariri glass towers." Abu Sami was referring to an Islamic cemetery located in Beirut's downtown area that had been bulldozed by Solidere to make room for new development. When the war ended, Abu Sami not only lost his business in the downtown area; he could not stop Solidere from wiping out the tombs of his parents and relatives. Abu Sami expressed his dissatisfaction with Solidere's plans by ranting to his customers. He and a few of his customers often vented their frustration by discussing politics and making sarcastic jokes about politicians.

Other city residents challenged their exclusion from the future plans of the city by claiming historical or religious attachment to specific urban locales. Members of marginal groups constructed "imaginary geographies" that allowed them to compete against other groups over symbolic urban sites. Architect Jad Tabet[20] described an incident where four competing religious communities fought over the layers of an archaeological site located at the heart of Beirut's Central District. When archaeologists carried out a salvage dig after Solidere demolished a large building, the layers close to the surface revealed what seemed to be a mosque or a shrine. The Sunnis claimed the site, demanded that that specific archaeological layer be preserved, and mobilized to stop the dig. A few days later, news of the shrine reached the Shi'ite community, which believed the shrine contained the remains of a Shi'ite religious figure. For several days, young members of Hizballah came to the site to manage the crowds of Shi'ites who arrived to pay homage. The archaeological site then became the center of conflict between the two parties. The Sunnis considered themselves among the original residents of Beirut and viewed the Shi'ites as outsiders because of their rural origins. A few days after the Shi'ites took control of the site, the Mufti, (the highest Sunni Muslim religious authority in Lebanon), issued a religious decree stating that the shrine housed the tomb of a Sunni religious teacher and it did not belong to the Shi'ites. The archaeologists continued their dig. The next archaeological layer revealed a Byzantine structure with mosaic floors. This time, a number of women from the Greek Orthodox Christian community demonstrated at the site and called for the archaeologists to discontinue the dig. Similar to the Sunnis, the Greek Orthodox community considered themselves among the original residents of Beirut. Finally, the Maronite Christians, who migrated to the city from rural areas, wanted the archaeologists to dig deeper, assuming they would reach a Phoenician layer.

Each of the religious communities claimed attachment to the city's past. The Sunnis, the Shi'ites, the Greek Orthodox, and the Maronites all wanted the archaeological excavations to stop at the layer where their imagined past was represented. By claiming a specific archaeological layer, each community was implicitly denying other communities the right to identify themselves with the city's past. Despite the fights over the archaeological site, none of these groups was able to preserve its claimed archaeological layer. The minute the archaeologists left the site, Solidere's bulldozers flattened the area to make way for new high-rise buildings.

The increasing interest in claiming the city's past and preserving its heritage exacerbated the divisions among Lebanon's eighteen ethnoreligious groups. Each group fought to advocate for itself and to prove that its past should be valued and maintained above the others. In *The Heritage Crusade and the Spoils of History*, David Lowenthal explained that communities believed "their heritage concerns to be unique, reflecting some trait of character or circumstance, some spirit of veneration or revenge that is peculiarly their own" (1998, 4). The interpretation of the past turned historic sites into politically charged issues. What was preserved depended on who made the choice and what they perceived history to be according to their own perspective (Tiesdell, Taner, and Heath 1996, 16).

Despite all of these fights, several attempts were made to construct a unified past. Lebanese intellectuals and concerned groups debated the meanings of heritage (*al-turath*), authenticity (*al-aṣala*), and modernity (*al-ḥadatha*). They worked to revive the "heritage" and maintain the "authentic" in order to pull together a unified people capable of facing external threats. In this context, the proponents of heritage sought to bring together the multiple ethnoreligious groups in a unified national frame.

Immediately after the war ended, the Lebanese held a conference to define "national heritage" and "popular culture." The "First Conference on Popular Culture in Lebanon" was held in December 1993. Terms such as "heritage" and "authenticity" were given a prominent place on the agenda. The participants in this convention were all figures of power: government ministers from an assortment of departments—including media, internal affairs, tourism, culture, and higher education; two members of parliament; the director of the Hariri Foundation; professors at local universities; and independent researchers and writers. At this gathering, the participants discussed what constituted the nation's heritage. In the end, they failed to reach an agreement. Nonetheless, in his report, Lebanese journalist and writer Joseph Basil wrote that despite their differences, these intellectuals shared a definition of Lebanon's popular heritage as "the accumulation of the experiences of ordinary people, experiences that stretched over thousands of years through the many successive governments and armies" (1994, 135–136). In an attempt to include all strata of society within a collective vision, the participants agreed that their heritage should have four characteristics: collective, unique, divergent, and multifold. To accomplish this vision, they recommended that the state, with its cultural and academic institutions, play a key role in collecting and preserving not only the country's heritage but also its popular culture. In this move, heritage was conflated with yet another complex category, popular culture.

The conference reporter, Basil, acknowledged the variations in the components of heritage among distinct Lebanese groups. Moreover, he attributed these differences to geographic regions rather than to sectarian or religious affiliation, that is, to rural (agrarian and generally more poor) or urban (cosmopolitan and modern) differences. This was a notable assertion, given that it came after a long civil war that was based largely on sectarian divisions — not on regional differences. According to this vision, heritage transcended sectarian affiliations but not social classes. When the conference participants attempted to obscure the still-volatile tensions between different religious identities, they defined "heritage" in a way that would help the process of recovering from the war.

In an attempt to create a national heritage (nonexistent before the war), the attendees discussed rural traditions that were "believed" to constitute a national heritage that would unite the once-fighting factions. Highlighting the elements that ostensibly unified the nation induced a collective amnesia in which the various sectarian "traditions" were now silenced.

The task became one of deciding which practices were remembered and which were deliberately to be forgotten. The aspects of heritage highlighted by the powerful voices were mostly *rural nonsectarian* practices. These cultural practices were shared by all religious and sectarian groups who lived in the same geographical region: Christians, Druze, and Muslims. Basil argued for a geographic, nonsectarian scheme and stated that the Christians shared the same popular heritage as the Druze, because both groups had lived in the Chūf Mountains, while the "tribal mentality" of the Shi'ites in the Hermil region was shared by the Maronite Christians in the Bshirī area. Conference speakers, who were mostly city dwellers, invoked a shared past, one that belonged to rural traditions. Ironically, the rural population believed to practice these traditions was absent from the convention. Officials and intellectuals called for collecting, preserving, restoring, and replicating proverbs, songs, fables, marriage traditions, and, interestingly, religious rituals. Government officials and the elite wanted to safeguard selective aspects of ordinary people's lifestyles. To preserve these cultural forms, the elite appropriated the traditions of the rural population as the public property of the nation's unified past.

These official voices expressed a growing desire to promote a national collective heritage that could be shared by Lebanon's eighteen ethnoreligious groups. However, this vision of a unified heritage failed to address ethnic and religious differences. The phrase "elite culture" was used to refer to urban traditions as opposed to rural culture, a distinction that raised contradictions, as I explain later. A close examination of the proceedings of the convention reveals that despite what Basil reported, the participants in fact reached no consensus on the definitions of these key terms: "culture" (*thaqafa*), "popular culture" (*thaqafa sha'abiya*), "tradition" (*taqalīd*), "heritage" (*turath*), and "elite culture" (*thaqafat al-nukhba*). Although the definition of heritage was contested, nonetheless it was agreed that whatever it was, it must be preserved. More emphatically, it was decided that collecting the heritage, traditions, and memories of the Lebanese people should be a national priority.

Debates on authenticity, modernity, and the importance of protecting the country's heritage were not unique to Lebanon. These issues were part of an ongoing discussion in neighboring Arab countries. For example, Mohammad Tahan (1993), in an article documenting the proceedings of a conference held in Syria titled "Reading the Heritage: The Open Text and the Closed Text," also discussed the multiple meanings of heritage and the importance of restoring, preserving, or rejecting certain aspects of the past. He defined heritage (*al-turath*) as "what was produced in the past and continues to exist among us in the present. It is the cultural memory we keep either consciously or mythically as Arabs, Muslims, and human beings" (Tahan 1993, 39). He believed that Arab thought is in crisis and argued that heritage is not the problem of the past, but rather it is the problem of the present through which Arabs pursue the future.

It is logical to ask why and how heritage became a matter of concern in Lebanon. The postwar state of emergency in Beirut placed its residents in a situation where they were uncertain of their own present and the future of the city and the country. Many doubted the political promises and the reconstruction plans. They found themselves excluded from the future plans of the postwar city, and many were afraid they would not be able to continue to live there. In response to this state of uncertainty, the past was idealized as a refuge from an unpredictable future. They turned to a familiar past that was far from the unpleasant present and the unknown future.

ELECTION LANGUAGE
INCORPORATES RECONSTRUCTION

Colorful posters and banners that promoted parliamentary candidates covered hundreds of walls, lampposts, entrances of private and public buildings, shop windows, and even trees. Election blurbs invited residents to vote for the doctor, the engineer, the lawyer, and the educator who promised to work hard to end corruption associated with construction, to fight nepotism and sectarianism, and to heal the wounds of the war-torn city. The following examples of the 1996 parliamentary election material highlight the centrality of reconstruction:

> He is concerned about bulldozing our ruins and history in the name of reconstruction. He is the one who stepped in front of the bulldozers to protect the history of Beirut . . .
> In addition to his belief in the need for a museum for the ruins, he is calling for establishing a special museum for the city of Beirut. (From the 1996 election campaign of Mohamad Kabbani)

> His major concerns are: liberating the occupied land, repairing the educational system, and supporting the reconstruction project so Beirut becomes the place to which all cities direct their prayers (*qiblat al-mada'in*). (From the 1996 election campaign of Hussein Ali Yatim)

> The marriage between authority and money in the 1996 elections will only produce a large number of "illegal children." This is not acceptable in twentieth-century democracies. . . . It is not true that sectarianism is dividing the Lebanese, because they all praise one god, which is money.
> We all should be alert to this era . . . the era of the bulldozers and steamroller (*maḥdale*). . . . At this time, we cannot leave it for the drivers of the bulldozers to slow the destruction machines. If we let this hap-

pen, we will cause lots of harm to the history of our city. (Interview with Isam Numan after he lost the 1996 election)[21]

Thus politicians often justified their candidacy in relation to their position toward Solidere. While supporters argued that the reconstruction plan was the only viable option to build a modern city, opponents accused the project of destroying Beirut's heritage and expressed their willingness to challenge Solidere by all means, including blocking the bulldozers with their own bodies. The reconstruction project shaped the vocabulary of Beirut's inhabitants as well as its political leaders. Media and news agencies used words such as "bulldozer" and "steamroller" to describe Prime Minister Rafik Hariri and the Speaker of the Parliament, Nabih Berri. Later on, these same leaders appropriated this criticism and described themselves as construction machines to suggest their own strength and power. Hariri followers warned the public that he would bulldoze all of his opponents if he needed to.

Rafik Hariri spearheaded the reconstruction process and proudly described Beirut as "a big construction site" (*warcha kabira*) and named his electoral assembly the Group of Development and Construction (*kutlat al-inma' wa -al-i'mar*). In response to accusations of neglecting people's needs, Hariri's assembly adopted the slogan "Rebuilding Humans and Stones" (*bina' al-bashar wa-al-hajar*).

Despite Hariri's claims to "rebuild both humans and stones," Solidere's project isolated Beirut's Central District from the rest of the city and alienated its residents from what was once a familiar landscape. After Solidere launched its rebuilding project, Beirutis started to refer to the area as "al-Solidere" and stopped using its prewar and wartime name of "the Downtown" (al-Balad). In an attempt to reintroduce the marginalized residents to the newly constructed BCD area, Solidere organized occasional public functions at which the past and the present intertwined. These functions included Beirut's Annual Arabic Book Exhibit, a monthly flea market, the International Industrial Exhibit, and the Sphinx Nights, each of which I describe briefly.

In the spring of 1997, Beirut's Annual Arabic Book Exhibit opened for the first time since the eruption of the war in 1991.[22] Publishers from Lebanon and other Arab countries displayed their books in a huge tent set up in the middle of the reconstruction site, where authors signed their newly released books.

In addition to the book exhibit, Solidere revived another public function. Before the war, one of the commercial areas in Beirut's Central

District was named the Flea Market (Souq al-Barghouth), but Solidere demolished this old bazaar and instead hosted a monthly flea market at the same tent used for the book exhibit. In this market, antique dealers presented their goods, which ranged from expensive eighteenth-century European furniture to Orientalist paintings to old tools and antique jewelry.

To celebrate the future, the International Industrial Exhibit Maʿarad al-Sinaʿat al-Dawli was held in the same tent. In this exhibit, export and import companies displayed construction materials and building equipment from different countries, while real estate companies and brokers sold and advertised apartments and houses in various parts of Lebanon.

At all of these activities vendors sold traditional Lebanese foods and drinks from stands that carried names of well-known prewar restaurants and snack shops. The owners printed the phrase "previously located in the downtown area" under the names of their stands to demonstrate authenticity and a vast expertise in the business. Although the food stands were hosted in Solidere's tent, the owners wanted to assure themselves that they once served their customers in the BCD area. One of the owners painfully compared his experience selling snacks in the temporary tent to that of his father and grandfather, who had owned a snack shop before the war. He complained that he was unable to establish a relationship with regular customers, and it saddened him that previous customers stopped by to recount their memories of when they frequented the shop before the war.

URBAN PLANS AND THE SHAPING OF SPACE

Any community claims its own history, and it is often impossible to locate a single narrative for a contested past. Each group within a community reconstructs its past with selective images that suit its present needs and future ambitions. Edward Said states that "daily anxieties and agendas have extraordinary influence on the images we construct of a privileged, genealogically useful past, a past in which we exclude unwanted elements, vestiges, narratives" (1993, 15). Socioeconomic factors and political conditions affect the ways the past is narrated through the process of including or excluding specific experiences. Michel Foucault (1977b) suggests that historians should understand the rhetorical context within which the politics of memory become constituted. For Foucault, the past is continually being remodeled in our present discourse about the future. What is remembered about the past depends on the way it is represented, which has to do with the power of groups in constructing their representation

(Foucault 1977b, 152–160). Each group recalls specific moments of its claimed past in which its members defended their rights, property, and space. These moments become sites of nostalgia, while others become sites of amnesia and are abolished from the daily vocabulary and collective memories.

Urban planning may be seen as a form of spatial domination and control of the ways communities construct their past and narrate their collective memories. It is a confrontation between urban social movements, planners, and politically and economically dominant regimes. How pivotal is the role of the state as a hegemonic force that limits the choices of people? How do various groups develop their agendas regarding the future and the past (Williams 1989)? Oren Yiftachel (1995) presents the political confrontation over space between the Israeli government and the Palestinian ethnic minority in Galilee, where planners and politicians enforce repression and fragmentation in the name of urban reform and development. In the case of postwar Beirut, it is the international and regional investors and developers who shaped histories, memories, and urban landscapes. In fact, Hariri commercialized national heritage and turned city spaces into commodities.

In postwar Beirut, the competition over urban places and spaces played a crucial role in shaping social and political relations in the city. Here I would argue that space became a resilient concept, by which I mean a non-fixed or a fluid notion. There were attempts to fix urban spaces by textualizing certain landscapes (neighborhoods, buildings, and monuments) by considering them historically valuable for the whole nation, which meant attaching history to them. This is clear through what is called "place attachment," creating imaginary geographies that allow particular sites to become associated with certain values, historical events, and feelings. This leads us to Foucault's concept of "heterotopias," the designation of places "outside of all places . . . places which are absolutely different from all sites that [people] reflect and speak about" (1986, 24). Pointing to the importance of constructed cultural meanings that influence the perception of the places in which people live, Setha Low (1994, 1996) argues that there is a difference between the cultural values, rules, and perspectives of people who design and build housing and those who use it.

In Beirut, Solidere fixed sites by institutionalizing them as historical monuments. Solidere's project changed the physical structures and the functions of buildings and alienated the residents from their surroundings. Places that once were familiar became foreign and perhaps prohibited. An episode concerning a conference in the United States demonstrates this inverted reality.

In April 1997, Solidere and the Graduate School of Design at Harvard University organized a conference entitled "Projecting Beirut." In the exhibition associated with the conference, posters, slides, and maps presented images of the future downtown Beirut. The images portrayed a negative image of reality. The downtown area was projected as colorful and lively, a place where small boats sailed in the peaceful water, pedestrians dressed in colorful clothes, lovely cafés were filled with customers, and plenty of open green spaces were provided. The rest of the city (on the maps and posters) was portrayed as colorless, empty, and without any signs of life. At first glance, an observer would believe the downtown area was full of life while the rest of the city was dead and empty. In reality, the downtown area was physically "empty" of any kind of urban activity except for a number of trucks and bulldozers and construction workers wearing Solidere-labeled hard hats.

Spaces that are labeled empty can hold a multiplicity of meanings. Gary McDonogh (1993) sees emptiness as going beyond the designation of open urban lands to denote those spaces that are undefined, or those in which the definition is indistinct because of unresolved conflicts over meaning. The emptiness that McDonogh suggests has crucial significance in urban areas, where "empty spaces" are charged with meaning.

Although Solidere portrayed the future downtown as full of life and the rest of the city as dead and empty, residents of Beirut employed the concept of empty space in other contexts. When people talked about the dramatic Israeli invasion of Beirut in 1982, the streets and the city itself were described as being empty, although Israeli tanks and soldiers occupied the streets. In other contexts, emptiness was used as a desired concept. Beirutis who remained in the city during the war spoke proudly of their efforts to keep the apartments of neighbors and relatives empty, thereby protecting them from being occupied by the war-displaced or by militiamen. Empty places were culturally and socially meaningful in all kinds of city narratives. Some people described the neighborhoods when they first moved to them—forty or fifty years ago—as "empty," meaning that these neighborhoods were not as crowded then as they were at the time they told me their stories. The people wanted to prove they played a role in establishing the area and witnessed its growth by not making it "empty." In other situations, when telling the history of a particular neighborhood, the narrator often excluded certain groups of people by

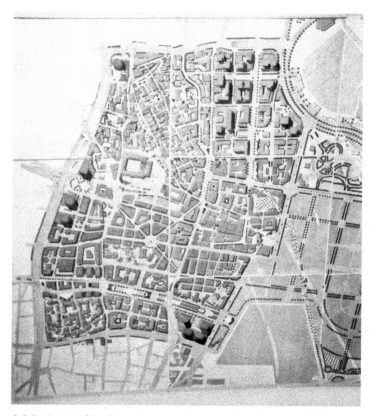

Solidere's map of the future downtown Beirut. In the color version, the concentrated areas are colored in vibrant hues while the rest of the city is left in dull colors.

referring to an area as "empty." In such narratives, the speakers excluded and even did not see other users of the same spaces.

CONCLUDING REMARKS

The top-down project of rebuilding downtown Beirut, carried out by international investors and Lebanon's political elite, resulted in heated debates among developers, urban planners, property owners, intellectuals, historians, social scientists, and the political opposition. Because Solidere's priority was to construct modern structures that would compete in the global markets, those who opposed the plans feared that the future city would lose its identity, and they accused the reconstruction company of disconnecting Beirut from its multilayered past and argued that the needs of ordinary Beirutis were being ignored. To accommodate its critics, Solidere designated a few buildings as "historically valuable." An atmosphere of uncertainty engulfed the project and permeated ordinary life in the city. Although Solidere's project was centered in Beirut's Central District, its unpredictable consequences extended to neighboring areas as it changed people's relation to space.

The chapters that follow shift across different groups and their respective sites to explore how each was affected by this postwar transformation of space. I begin, in the next chapter, with legal residents and their long-time apartments.

In the previous chapter I discussed debates that emerged in response to Solidere's plans to rebuild Beirut's Central District. I now trace the effects of reconstruction on the daily lives of the residents of 'Ayn el-Mreisse, an adjacent neighborhood. This chapter illustrates the postwar temporality at the local community level. It explores the uncertain relationship between wartime tenants and property owners and details the ways postwar emergencies affected the relationships between family members, neighbors, old and new residents, and political groups of 'Ayn el-Mreisse. In the aftermath of the war, with the physical space changing constantly, the lives of the area's inhabitants were on hold, resources were unstable, and no one seemed to know clearly "how to play the game," that is, how to negotiate urban spaces and rights. While property owners deliberated about whether to sell their estates to investors and developers, their tenants had to find alternative housing. Similarly, the displaced population had to negotiate compensation for agreeing to evacuate commercial and residential buildings they had occupied during the war. Since there were many parties involved in the rebuilding process, residents of this neighborhood found it difficult to locate the right governmental agency or private institution to appeal to in the long process of securing urban rights.

In 'Ayn el-Mreisse, a multi-ethnoreligious neighborhood, each group had a different vision of how to rebuild and conserve specific sections of the area. Each group constructed its own maps delineating the borders of the neighborhood. Additionally, each group invoked specific spatial experiences to prove its right to contested city spaces and denied the same right to other competing groups.

CHANGING LANDSCAPES

Riding the *sarvees*[1] car through 'Ayn el-Mreisse in the late 1990s, one encountered multiple landscapes and spaces. The *sarvees* car drove along

Hizballah drum band marching on Corniche Street, officially named Rue de Paris

Corniche Street, officially named Rue de Paris, a street that separates the neighborhood from the sea, then moved uphill into narrower streets and alleys. Along the eastern side of Corniche stood old houses, restaurants, food stands, grocery stores, hotels, and car shops. Construction materials and machinery blocked the sidewalks and even part of the streets. Numerous new buildings had already been erected, and many others were under construction. Huge colored banners draped on the newly constructed towers illustrated the future finished buildings and advertised the availability of luxury apartments and offices, as well as the responsible engineering firm, the real estate agent, the elevator company, and the property owners.

The passengers of the *sarvees* openly exchanged stories, engaged in political discussions, and made jokes. Very often, when the *sarvees* passed one of the new buildings, a passenger would make a comment about how the investors were in the habit of illegally building these luxurious apartments and offices. They described the investors as warlords or as outsiders and explained the source of funding as coming from "oil money or Gulf States dollars (*dollarat al*-Khaleej) or money from Africa!"[2] These statements were usually followed by a moment of silence as the speaker waited for a response from his fellow riders. Once, a middle-aged man who sat next to the driver commented: "These buildings are not built for the Lebanese, or for those of us who protected the city during the war. On the contrary, they are constructed by strangers for other strangers." A new passenger got into the *sarvees* and immediately engaged in the ongoing discussion, stating, "I just lost $10,000 to one of those thieves who called himself an investor. He [the investor] promised the depositors high interest rates for investing the money in construction. I gave him my life savings, and now I cannot find him; he vanished. I heard rumors that he had left the country." Other passengers sympathized with him, saying that they had heard of similar stories, and assured the man that God would compensate him with patience and serenity. Such conversations were expressions of disapproval toward the rebuilding projects and of the helplessness of ordinary people to take part in the reconstruction of their city.

Among the gigantic newly constructed buildings stood a number of shorter buildings known as the traditional Beiruti houses (*buyūt bayrut al-taqlidiya*). The traditional yellow sandstone houses generally consisted of two to four floors roofed with red tiles, with balconies overlooking the streets, and were surrounded by small walled gardens. The walls and the houses themselves were scarred by bullet holes that seemed part of their original architectural design. Some walls were patched here and there to fill in bullet punctures and rocket cracks. Their gardens usually contained a marble fountain surrounded by lemon, fruit, and jasmine trees as well as beds of herbs and flowers. According to the residents of ʿAyn el-Mreisse, these houses were built for upper- and middle-class city merchants between the 1920s and the 1950s by European architects and designers. Less than a century old, and built to resemble French-style architecture, the "traditional Beiruti house" had over time become a valuable and endangered symbol of the city's past. A number of local nongovernmental organizations took it upon themselves to preserve these old houses and declared them historical landmarks.[3] In ʿAyn el-Mreisse, some of these houses were occupied by their original owners or by displaced families, and a few were used by the Syrian army as military posts. The passengers who condemned the new buildings never discussed the nearby old houses occupied by the Syrian army. In fact, the *sarvees* passengers had erased these spaces from their mental maps, especially in the presence of distrusted strangers. Until the withdrawal of Syria's fourteen thousand troops from Lebanon in 2005, the Lebanese were vigilant about expressing their dissatisfaction with the Syrian intervention in their country.[4] In public places and in the presence of strangers, most Beirutis were worried that a Syrian secret agent might be lurking. Nonetheless, in private gatherings of trusted friends and family members, they always criticized, debated, and made political jokes about the Syrian army. Ironic nicknames such as "the brothers" (*al-ashiqa'*) or the newly constructed word "enemy-friends" (*al-'adiqa'*) were used to refer to the Syrians.[5]

Next, the *sarvees* drove over an underground tunnel that connected the campus of American University of Beirut (AUB) to its privately owned beach. AUB had blocked its seashore with a straw fence. A *sarvees* passenger ridiculed the fence and said "The American University has veiled the beach to protect its naked girls from the eyes of the passersby." Later on, the *sarvees* passed a large empty lot surrounded by metal walls. These walls were chaotically covered with layers of colorful posters for political groups, movies, nightclubs, singers, and dancers. That was once the site of the American Embassy, blown up during the war in April 1983. Although the embassy did not physically exist there anymore, residents gave directions in relation to the embassy as if it were still standing. They would say "the house is located behind the American Embassy," or "turn left after you pass the embassy's entrance."

The car traveled on a small, old bridge overlooking 'Ayn el-Mreisse's fishing port. On one side of the bridge there were shacks and a few fishing boats turned upside down, and alongside the shacks stood a gigantic building under construction. The fishing port was appropriated by investors with the goal of building a luxurious apartment building called the Dreams Building (Binayat al-Aḥlam). Side by side, the fishermen as well as other neighborhood residents protested the new building and fought to preserve 'Ayn el-Mreisse's fishing port, since it was the only one remaining in West Beirut.

An old Ottoman mosque stood on the same side of the street. At the intersection between Corniche Street and the street facing the mosque there was an enormous concrete flat triangle with a fading black-and-white print of Jamal Abdul-Nasser, Egypt's charismatic president during the 1950s and 1960s. Although the structure was not a statue, area residents fondly referred to it as Nasser's statue (*timthal* Nasser), or simply "the statue," a nostalgic symbol of Arab nationalism and identity.

In addition to these three landmarks that represented Arab and Islamic identity, the mosque, Nasser's statue, and the fishing port, the Hard Rock Cafe has occupied one of the new buildings since 1997. The walls of the building were decorated with a shiny twelve-meter-high red glass guitar and two murals of a young man and a woman in Western clothes standing in a red phone booth. Across the street stood a prewar abandoned structure made of wide, rusty metal arches. Area residents referred to it as the House of the Lebanese Craftsman (Bayt al-Muḥtarif al-Lubnanī).[6] Adjacent to the metal structure, two prewar beaches continued to be used: "'Ajram Beach" for women and children, and "the French Beach" for both men and women. Next to the beaches stood the newly built Lebanese Artisanat, where "traditional Lebanese" crafts were marketed to affluent Lebanese and tourists.

As the *sarvees* drove away from the seaside toward a steep, narrow street, the newly renovated Beirut Theater could be seen with its wide, arched wood-and-brass door. Its entrance was decorated with posters of the upcoming activities and events. In the narrow side streets, there were cars parked on both sides of the road and sometimes on the sidewalks as well. Traffic was halted as a driver stepped out of his idling car to purchase a beverage, while other cars honked and the drivers cursed each other.

The inner alleys and narrow roads of 'Ayn el-Mreisse were flanked by small, old cement houses with narrow balconies overlooking the bustling streets. Construction workers repaired old buildings, added new floors and balconies,[7] and patched bullet holes. Hundreds of electric wires dangled from the buildings' roofs and windows, and these wires connected apartments to more than one private source of electricity.[8] On both sides of the street there were butcher shops, bakeries, grocery stores, small clothing boutiques, and restaurants. At the end of the alley stood a temporary vegetable market housed in makeshift shacks and run by young Kurdish men. Unemployed men wandered the area; others sat on folding chairs in parking lots and in front of shops, where they played cards and backgammon, talked, and listened to music. Housewives shopped at the vegetable market and the butcher shop while children played on the sidewalks and between the passing cars. Neighbors usually talked to shopkeepers and other neighbors and called down to people in the street from their balconies.

On an even narrower street, parallel to Corniche, there were a number of poorly renovated apartment buildings that carried English names such as "The Broadway," "The Gulf Tower," and "The Star." After the evacuation of the war-displaced, the owners returned these apartments to their prewar functions and rented them to single male students and women prostitutes who worked at the nightclubs and bars on Martínez Street, the street known as the red-light district of prewar Beirut.

Throughout the neighborhood, the walls of commercial and residential buildings and the balconies of private apartments were covered with posters, banners, and signs that advertised seasonal festivities, religious ceremonies, and political activities. During parliamentary elections, candidates competed among themselves and negotiated with property

One of 'Ayn el-Mreisse's many alleys decorated with political posters

A narrow street in the 'Ayn el-Mreisse neighborhood

owners and local political leaders to prominently post their smiling photo posters and other electoral materials. During the holy Muslim month of Ramadan, rival political groups decorated the streets with their banners, flags, and lights to remind their constituencies of fasting and to assert the presence of Muslim life in the neighborhood. During the Shi'ite ceremony of 'Ashura',[9] the two major Shi'ite religion-based political parties, Amal Movement and Hizballah, asserted their control over the area and hung black and green banners with verses from the Quran, sayings of the Prophet Mohammad, mottos of the Shi'ite leaders, and other political statements. These banners signaled the ongoing competition for control in the area: the group with more banners had more followers and power.

The politically marked structures, the war-scarred buildings, the decorated surfaces, and the polished new buildings encountered when driving through 'Ayn el-Mreisse represented the various social groups that competed for the control of space. While investors and developers erected large buildings, local residents preserved some of the old ones and deployed their political and religious symbols as they competed over claims to authenticity and legitimacy. This competition among the prewar, wartime, and postwar users of space was manifested in the ways various groups and individuals recalled their prewar and wartime spatial experiences.

MAJOR POWER STRUCTURES IN 'AYN EL-MREISSE

The changes in the landscape of 'Ayn el-Mreisse were accompanied by dramatic changes in the power hierarchies among its old and new residents. In addition to the transformation in the roles and responsibilities of the wartime political actors such as militias and religious and political groups, new economic and institutional entities entered the existing power hierarchy. In what follows, I map out the major influential actors whose plans, strategies, and actions directly and indirectly shaped the lives of the local residents of 'Ayn el-Mreisse.

Generally speaking, there are four major blocs of interest and power in 'Ayn el-Mreisse. One is made up of the political parties, which have evolved out of wartime sects and militias. Membership is mainly based on religious and ideological affiliation. Second are the revived governmental institutions, such as the Municipality of Beirut, and the newly formed ones, such as the Ministry of the Displaced. The third actor is Solidere, the real estate reconstruction company in charge of rebuilding the downtown area. Fourth are the financial forces, which include regional and international investors and developers.

While the government tried to reactivate its institutions and resume its responsibilities after two decades of absence, wartime militias, political parties, and traditional leadership competed with the postwar stakeholders, regional and international developers and investors, to take part in the postwar efforts of reconstruction. Political parties modified their goals, priorities, and strategies to accommodate the needs of their members. For example, the Shi'ite Amal Movement and the Hizballah party that controlled 'Ayn el-Mreisse during the war now resorted to new means to recruit followers. Both parties continued to provide area residents with some services and negotiated with state institutions and private developers on behalf of their followers. Ironically, members of some of these wartime political groups and militias were appointed as ministers in the new government. Wartime militia leaders who became postwar high-ranking officials could also be found among the powerful developers and investors.[10] This overlap in roles and confusion about the responsibilities among the power brokers—political parties, financial agents, and governmental institutions—forced Beirutis to utilize creative means and strategies to access information and secure their rights to city spaces and services.

SOLIDERE

As discussed in Chapter Two, Solidere's activities were supposed to be limited to the downtown area. However, the residents of 'Ayn el-Mreisse were worried that Solidere's project would expand westward and take over parts of their neighborhood. In fact, Solidere had already confiscated some properties in 'Ayn el-Mreisse when it built a highway and a 3.6 km ring road that connected the downtown area to the airport. Although Solidere claimed that its "massive and global reconstruction of the war-torn city center was seen as a must-do action to announce the end of war and the beginning of return to normality" (Kabbani 1996, 8), its responsibilities toward local residents were not clearly defined. 'Ayn el-Mreisse residents complained that although it was Solidere that confiscated their land, the residents' paperwork was the responsibility of other state agencies such as the Municipality of Beirut, the Ministry of Public Works, and the Central Fund for the Displaced. Yet the local residents did not know which agency they should address and on what basis.

In addition to appropriating property in the area, Solidere's project caused real estate values to sky-rocket in 'Ayn el-Mreisse. Because of the neighborhood's proximity to the downtown area, the value its land had, in fact, tripled. The sudden rise in property values and the increasing demand for land complicated residents' relationships to their familiar spaces and intensified the state of uncertainty and unpredictability they experienced in the postwar era.

THE MUNICIPALITIES OF BEIRUT

In the aftermath of the war, the Municipality of Beirut tried to reclaim its rights and responsibilities, which proved difficult. With few resources to draw upon, officials used various means to collect unpaid debts from residents who had not paid any fees or taxes for the past twenty years: the duration of the war and its immediate aftermath.

During the war, the building that housed the municipality in the downtown area was abandoned. Two temporary sites for municipality offices were created, one in the Christian east side and the other across the Green Line in the Muslim west side of the city. The two municipality sites provided minimum services and were closed most of the time. After the war, the municipality continued to operate from its two rental buildings, and the mayor (*ra'is al-baladiya*) divided his time between the two locations. The municipality was united when it was relocated to its renovated permanent location in the downtown area.

In the postwar era, Beirutis had to deal again with governmental institutions and bureaucracies such as the municipality. For example, the municipality refused to issue birth and death certificates, personal identification cards, building permits, and other documents until the applicants paid their accumulated past-due debts. Additionally, the municipality granted a two-month grace period to property owners to obtain licenses for buildings constructed during the war or illegal structures such as balconies, floors, and garages added to pre-licensed buildings. The owners had to pay their past-due debts in addition to new registration fees and fines.

THE AMAL MOVEMENT

The Amal Movement is a Shi'ite political party that had risen to prominence in the 1980s (Norton 1987). During the war, Amal's militia controlled various neighborhoods throughout Beirut. By the late 1980s, Amal was one of the major service providers in 'Ayn el-Mreisse. It had generators distributing electricity, provided drinking water, operated a health clinic, and managed to house many of the Shi'ite war-displaced. Since there was no longer a need for its wartime services, Amal had lost the control and influence it had enjoyed earlier. Amal tried to retain some of its influence by empowering the Shi'ite community in the neighborhood and defending its rights by playing the role of an intermediary when it negotiated on their behalf.

Amal enjoyed popularity among the war-displaced Shi'ites, who were generally looked down upon and were accused by the nondisplaced of downgrading the neighborhood. Amal was in the process of building housing projects for its displaced followers in the Southern Suburb of Beirut. On many occasions, the Amal Movement extended its services to include the non-Shi'ite residents of 'Ayn el-Mreisse. When the Israelis bombed the main electricity generators of Beirut in 1996, for example, Amal temporarily provided electricity for many of the area residents through generators privately owned by its members.[11]

INVESTORS AND DEVELOPERS

Due to 'Ayn el-Mreisse's location next to the city center and the Mediterranean coast, land prices had already tripled in the two years immediately following the war (Tabet 1993). Old residential buildings were demolished and replaced with modern towers for office space and high-income residents. Sociologist Nabil Beyhum estimated that more than two hundred companies from Western and Arab countries took part in rebuilding Beirut (Beyhum et al. 1992). Regional investors, mostly from the Arab Gulf countries, and diasporic Lebanese investors purchased land in 'Ayn el-Mreisse to open chain restaurants, international hotels, and entertainment facilities. In December of 1997, the Hard Rock Cafe celebrated its opening in the presence of Prime Minister Rafik Hariri and a number of businessmen.

The new apartments and offices, rumored to be sold for several million dollars each, were beyond the means of the residents of 'Ayn el-Mreisse. Consequently, local area residents found themselves forced to sell their property and relocate to other areas. Those who decided to stay found themselves strangers in their own neighborhoods.

CONSTRUCTING MULTIPLE MAPS: NAMES AND BORDERS

In the postwar era, 'Ayn el-Mreisse's physical borders, maps, history, and name became contested domains among its residents. Investors and developers, the municipality, and old and new residents constructed conflict-

A mural of the logo of the Amal Movement, the Shi'ite political party, on the side of a building in 'Ayn el-Mreisse

ing borders, drew different maps, and told multifarious stories about the history and the name of the neighborhood. In day-to-day life, residents never used the municipality's official name, Dar al-Mreisse; instead they used the local name, 'Ayn el-Mreisse. They justified and proved the originality of this name by telling me the following story:

A long time ago, a boat that carried nuns sank in the sea. A lucky nun survived and managed to swim safely to the shore. She stayed next to the water spring in the neighborhood and lit candles to thank God for saving her life. The curious children of the fishermen who lived around the spring came to see the nun. She taught them reading and writing. To express their appreciation, the fishermen built the nun a room next to the spring, and gave her the title of Rayseh [female chief of the fishermen]. Since then, the neighborhood came to be called 'Ayn el-Mreisse, or "the spring of fisherwoman chief."

Even so, the borders of 'Ayn el-Mreisse were still contested. The neighborhood's administrative boundaries were different from the borders described by the residents. According to the municipal map, 'Ayn el-Mreisse was located between the Ras Beirut area to the east, the American University of Beirut to the south, and the seashore boulevard, known as Rue de Paris, to the west. Neighborhood residents rejected the municipal borders and considered different boundaries, and each constructed varying mental maps. In interviews with current and previous residents of the neighborhood, some included the entire area of Ras Beirut, others incorporated segments of the downtown area, a third group claimed the American University of Beirut, and a fourth group included only a few of the area's inner streets. But none of them used the municipality's official name, Dar el-Mreisse, nor its administrative borders.

Unlike the other residents, the fishermen offered yet another configuration for the area. For As'ad, a forty-year-old fisherman who had lived and worked in the area all of his life, "'Ayn el-Mreisse consisted of the fishing port, the Corniche Street, and the whole Mediterranean Sea. For us, the water is part of the neighborhood. . . . We face the sea and turn our backs to the land." Like As'ad, the fishermen, who were among the least powerful, contested their marginalization and declared the fishing port to be the most important marker in the area.

Politicians provided borders different from those of the fishermen. A former parliament member, who was born and raised in the neighborhood, identified himself as the son of 'Ayn el-Mreisse (Ibn 'Ayn el-Mreisse) and proclaimed himself the spokesman of the history of the area. He told me that he served the area and its residents during the war when he was a board member of local youth and educational associations, and he continued to advocate for the area after he was elected to the parliament as a Sunni representative. He assertively drew the borders of the area by saying:

Listen, I am the one who could tell you the real borders of 'Ayn el-Mreisse. It is the area that is located between the sea from the north, Bliss Street to the west, Clemenceau Street to the south, and Al-Ḥuson Port to the east. This is the real 'Ayn el-Mreisse. Do not listen to anybody who gives you other borders.

In this version of the boundaries, the AUB campus became part of the neighborhood, a perception perhaps motivated by the fact that the speaker himself was an AUB graduate. Although he did not live in the neighborhood at the time I interviewed him, he claimed connectedness to the area and, at the same time, disavowed the same right to others. Despite these explicit instructions from the parliament member, in what follows I use a rather flexible definition of the neighborhood.[12]

MULTIPLE IDENTITIES AND LOYALTIES

Along with the constant physical changes of the landscape and the power hierarchies, there were changes in the socioeconomic relations and the ethnoreligious structures of 'Ayn el-Mreisse's inhabitants. During the war, many of the area's residents were forced out of their homes as a result of fighting and, later on, of reconstruction. In response to the postwar state of emergency and unpredictability, prewar residents nostalgically recalled the times when the area was happily shared by the following ethnoreligious groups: Sunnis, Shi'ites, Druze, Greek Orthodox Christians, Armenians, and Kurds.[13] They all belonged to different socioeconomic classes, and they worked as merchants in the city center, daily laborers at the port, tour guides and taxi drivers, waiters at nearby hotels, owners of souvenir shops, civil servants at governmental agencies, employees at AUB, and fishermen at the port.

During the war, militias and political parties, along with charitable organizations, replaced the malfunctioning state agencies. They provided housing for displaced families, distributed water and food, operated hospitals and health centers, ran schools, cleaned the streets, maintained shelters, and even provided safety and protection. To access these essential services, individuals were forced to align themselves with the militias who controlled their neighborhood.[14] Although many of the residents of 'Ayn el-Mreisse had joined several of the militias and sectarian political parties, they viewed these affiliations as temporary tactics and survival strategies. Many of the residents I interviewed argued that their loyalty to the neighborhood was stronger than their membership in political parties. Basim, who belonged to three militias during the war, reported that he maintained a close friendship with his childhood friends despite their memberships in rival militias. His uncle, who was present at the time of the interview, added: "There was an unspoken agreement among the young men of 'Ayn el-Mreisse to keep their political conflicts outside the area. When they were in the neighborhood, they knew they were no longer militia members. They had to leave their political affiliations and ideologies at their posts at the checkpoint." Contrary to Basim's uncle, other area residents told me stories about ethnoreligious conflicts among neighbors. For example, those who fought over property rights often sought the help of armed militiamen to threaten their lifelong neighbors.

Despite these memories of remembered sectarian frictions, the residents of 'Ayn el-Mreisse insisted that their loyalty to the neighborhood superseded their sectarian and religious connections. Nevertheless, a large number of studies on Lebanese society overestimate sectarian and religious belonging and underplay the importance of nonreligious alliances. For example, Fuad Khuri (1975) and Kamal Salibi (1988) criticized these studies for their failure to represent the complexity of Lebanese society. Similarly, Elizabeth Picard (1996) argued that client-patron relationships between the powerful and the powerless are fluid and are based on a multiplicity of social, political, economic, and historical factors, not simply militia alliances. As with the majority of Lebanese society, the residents of 'Ayn el-Mreisse used a combination of contradictory and complex alliances. For example, a family could seek help from a local sectarian leader (za'im) while at the same time take advantage of relationships with colleagues, friends, and neighbors to reach government officials. This combination of resources and usage of multiple alliances (sectarian and nonsectarian) created fluid rather than fixed identities. And yet, when asked about their sectarian affiliation, the residents of the neighborhood often criticized others for using sectarian connections to negotiate city privileges while simultaneously justifying their own occasional reliance on the power of these connections.

Even after the war, Beirutis were forced to continue relying on sectarian connections because their postwar government failed to provide them with the necessary urban services. City residents criticized the cabinet for its similarity to the wartime sectarian coalitions. They described the appointed ministers as warlords who "put down the war rifles and picked up reconstruction shovels."[15] 'Ayn el-Mreisse residents developed both temporary and long-term sectarian and nonsectarian interest groups to negotiate with the powerful postwar decision makers. For example, when the Ministry of the Displaced and private developers tried to evict Shiʿite families from their illegal homes, the targeted displaced population sought support from the two major Shiʿite political groups: the Amal Movement and Hizballah, as well as Sunni, Druze, Armenian, and other Christian associates.[16] Similarly, long-standing tenants who shared a building and who belonged to various religious groups worked together to buy electric generators, fix elevators, and even take landlords to court and force them to restore the building.

TENANTS AND LANDLORDS

The tension in the relationship between the long-standing tenants of ʿAyn el-Mreisse and property owners is an example of the "let's wait and see" phenomenon in which both sectarian and nonsectarian alliances were used. As property values escalated, landlords used both legal and illegal means available to them to evict prewar tenants who paid low rents. On the other hand, and in response to eviction notices, tenants negotiated higher compensation from their landlords, and an informal agreement called *khliw* was used to settle property disputes. In accordance with *khliw*, prewar tenants either qualified for a sum of money that was valued at less than half of the property's estimated price, or bought the dwelling for half of its estimated value. For example, an apartment worth $100,000 could be bought for $50,000, or a compensation of $40,000 was paid to the tenant for vacating.

The case of Nabil demonstrates this complex relationship between property owners and their prewar tenants. Nabil, a thirty-two-year-old Sunni Muslim, had lived in the same three-bedroom apartment since he was born. In fact, his parents had rented the apartment in 1960 before his birth. For many years, Nabil's family paid a reduced rent of $100 annually, while similar apartments were rented for $400–$500 a month. The landlord chose to sell the building for three million dollars to an investor who planned to demolish it in order to construct a hotel in its place. Then, in 1996, the landlord offered Nabil $30,000 as a *khliw* fee, but he turned it down and asked for $60,000. Later, a sum of $40,000 was offered. Nabil commented:

When I saw the landlord's lawyer, I proposed to buy the apartment for $40,000. Currently, I am unemployed, and I do not have the cash, but I know the owner is eager to sell the whole building. The investor won't buy the building with prewar tenants like me residing in it. By offering to buy the apartment, I hope the landlord agrees to pay me $50,000.

As Nabil waited for the compensation, his life was on hold. With the anticipated money, he hoped to make a down payment on a new apartment in the relatively affordable neighborhood of the Southern Suburb (al-Daḥiyya). He also planned on starting a small business, especially since he was unable to secure a job.

Usually, negotiations between owners and tenants were highly politicized and took a long time, because both parties employed a variety of negotiation tactics. Lawyers were hired to facilitate agreements. Sometimes, tenants shared the legal costs and negotiated either to keep their homes or to gain higher compensation (*khliw*). In addition to using lawyers, both landlords and tenants sometimes intimidated each other by threatening to use their connections to the Syrian military. Other property owners pressured occupants to leave the building by not providing services. Along with informal negotiations and the use of force, property owners also used other legal tactics to exert pressure. They either refused to accept the rent from their tenants, or they took the case to court if the tenant owned other property in the city or did not live permanently in the disputed apartment.

This strategy of "let's wait and see" extended from struggles between landlords and tenants to conflicts within households. Family members fought among themselves on how to spend the anticipated compensation. Unmarried sons wanted the money to pay for marriage expenses, unemployed family members hoped to start private businesses, mothers intended to move to areas close to their friends and relatives, and older men and women yearned to stay in the same home, since they resented leaving their familiar surroundings. Daughters, meanwhile, were pressured to give their shares of the profit to their brothers, regardless of their own needs. Um Jihad had lived in the same three-bedroom apartment for over forty years. Her eldest son, Jihad, his wife, and their two children lived in the largest room; her unemployed son, Ziad, and her disabled father occupied the second room; while she shared the third room with her two unmarried daughters. Um Jihad herself preferred to stay in the neighborhood close to her lifelong neighbors, but she made a compromise as her sons pressured her to accept the compensation and move out of the area. Um Jihad explained her plans:

With the money we will receive, God willing (*inshalah*), we will pay the first installment for two apartments in the Southern Suburb, one apartment for Jihad and his family and the second for the rest of us. We will give the rest of the money to Ziad, to buy a taxi. I hope my two daughters will get married soon and live on their own.

It took Um Jihad's family over six months to reach an agreement. Although Um Jihad herself would have preferred to stay where she had lived for the past forty years, she succumbed to the desires of her two sons. However, not all the family members were happy with the final compromise. Um Jihad's married daughter did not talk to her two brothers because they did not give her and her two unmarried sisters their share of the compensation money. Similar to what was happening in thousands of displaced families, the conflict over future places of residence and the plans for the anticipated compensation money affected the intimate relationships among family members.

CONCLUDING REMARKS

The atmosphere of uncertainty extended from the downtown area, where Solidere imposed its drastic reconstruction, to adjacent neighborhoods, and from commercial buildings to ordinary residences. This engendered a "let's wait and see" attitude among residents in 'Ayn el-Mreisse, which was manifested in the sour negotiations between long-standing tenants and landlords.

Because of real estate improvement, speculators invited property owners to sell their run-down buildings for high prices, which prompted owners to evict long-standing tenants. The tenants responded by negotiating either to leave with compensation or to be allowed to stay. This process intensified the state of unpredictability that characterized the reconstruction era. Tenants across many religious and ethnic affiliations formed temporary alliances, took their claims to court, and even sought the help of political groups and former militia members in their active response to eviction threats. In their arguments, tenants invoked the past, specifically their long history of living in the area, to support their demands.

Other groups used the past in similar ways, although for different kinds of spaces. The next chapter stays within the same neighborhood but shifts outside the context of the personal residence to examine collective responses to more public spaces under threat by redevelopment.

In Chapter Three, I mapped out the major postwar power actors who organized and appropriated space in ʿAyn el-Mreisse. In this chapter, I describe the formal and informal collectives organized to advocate for the rights of the less powerful residents to continue to have access to the spaces they had frequented before and during the war. Specifically, I examine the strategies, alliances, and tactics used by four groups that operated in the neighborhood: the fishermen of ʿAyn el-Mreisse, the Mosque Committee, the Association for the Revival of the Heritage of ʿAyn el-Mreisse, and the Beirut Theater collective. In contrast to groups generally documented in social-science writings about Lebanon, these collectives were nonsectarian in nature. Members of these collectives fought to maintain their spaces and to protect specific aspects of the neighborhood's heritage by relying on their recollection of places they cherished.

"THE SEA IS GOD'S PROPERTY": THE FISHERMEN

During my fieldwork, I worked closely with fishermen in ʿAyn el-Mreisse who mostly belonged to the Druze and Sunni sects. Until 1995, approximately fifty fishing boats operated out of the local fishing port.[1] Each of these boats provided work for three or four fishermen, who in turn supported 150–200 families. The number of fishermen dropped from eighty to forty after the port was appropriated by two private investors to construct the Dreams Building (Binayat al-Aḥlam,) a thirty-floor luxury residential tower. In response, the fishermen fought to preserve their right to fish from the port and relied heavily on their long history in the area. They proudly talked about their success in an earlier struggle against the municipal effort to build a highway and shut down the port.

Due to development projects initiated by the city and private investors, the size of the fishing port was reduced several times. In the 1960s and 1970s, the municipality confiscated the fishing port to make way for a major coastal highway that connected downtown Beirut to South Lebanon. With the support of the Workers' Union of Lebanon, the fishermen forced the municipality to alter its plans so as to maintain the port's functions. The fishermen credited their success to the strength of the unions, and they were specifically grateful to the head of the union, who was also the chief (*rayyes*) of the fishermen. The fishermen and their supporters obstructed the city's construction equipment and halted work on the highway for six months. When an agreement was finally reached to maintain the port, a bridge was then constructed to allow fishermen access to the water, and they were provided with enough space to keep their boats docked offshore. In exchange, the fishermen agreed to vacate their living quarters in shacks located in the vicinity of the port.

Unlike their relatively successful negotiations with the municipality in the 1970s, twenty years later the fishermen found themselves in a betwixt-and-between situation. They did not know how or against whom to protest, and they did not receive the support of the labor unions. Before the war, the fishing port was under the control of the Ministry of Agriculture. During the war, it became part of the Ministry of Transport and later the Ministry of Tourism, but in the aftermath of the war, the fishermen were unable to find a specific governmental agency in charge of their port. Because of this ambiguity about how to approach official channels, the fishermen mobilized all of their informal connections to preserve the fishing port. They formed alliances with local associations, contacted parliament members and influential politicians, involved the media, used both moral and legal arguments, and, as a last resort, spread rumors about the Dreams Building and its owners. They accused the investors of having bribed wartime government officials so they could illegally purchase the port. According to the fishermen, this transaction was a fraud because the contested land was officially designated as "sea property" (*amlak baḥreya*) and the fishermen deemed sea property "the property of God," hence no one was authorized to sell it, not even the government itself. According to the fishermen, the investors were guilty of violating official laws and of offending God himself when they denied the fishermen their source of income.

The fishermen continued their fight to preserve the port. They chose Abu 'Adnan al-Sayyad[2] as their spokesperson, as he was the chief fisherman, was considered the most experienced, and was trusted to work for the good of all the fishermen. Before the war, he had served as the president of the Lebanese Fishermen's Union and had led the negotiations with the municipality to save the port. Moreover, he had the time and fewer responsibilities, as he had neither a wife nor children to support. Every day, Abu 'Adnan sat from ten in the morning until midnight in front of his shack facing the newly constructed building. The yard in front of Abu 'Adnan's small room and the idle port offered a social space for the fishermen and their supporters to congregate. Visitors often sat there, played cards, smoked water pipes (*argileh*), and drank coffee. Upon the advice of his friends, Abu 'Adnan planned to write his memoirs about fishing in 'Ayn el-Mreisse as a way of documenting the area's threatened heritage.

One afternoon, while Abu 'Adnan and his clique played cards, a fisherman by the name of 'Abdo dashed toward them and happily announced that the Al-Aḥlam building was "sinking into the sea." The men turned their faces toward the gigantic structure, then asked 'Abdo for more details. After catching his breath, 'Abdo said the construction workers had told him that "the building sank five centimeters into the water because of an engineering error." Abu 'Adnan cheerfully commented, "Do you think God is asleep! No, He is up there watching out for us!" After they optimistically assured one another that the construction of the building would be halted, the fishermen sipped their coffee and returned to their cards.

Unlike the long-standing tenants of 'Ayn el-Mreisse who used the leases of their apartments to force property owners to pay them compensations, the fishermen did not possess any documents to legitimate their claims to the port. Instead, they used their memories of the port to legitimize their attachment to the place and to argue for their spatial rights. For example, the chief fisherman, Abu 'Adnan, asserted his rootedness to the area by demonstrating his thorough knowledge of seascapes (*tadaris al-baḥer*) and declaring that the sea was more important than the land. He said, "Although I lived here my entire life, my knowledge of the surrounding streets is far less than my knowledge of the water. For us, the fishermen, the sea is our permanent home. We usually face the sea and turn our backs to Beirut." The fishermen sincerely believed that their knowledge of the sea and their attachment to the fishing port should allow them to continue using it.

In addition to asserting their right to the fishing port through their acclaimed knowledge of the sea, the fishermen used other discourses when they sought popular support from neighbors, journalists, parliament candidates, and even anthropologists. For example, two neighborhood groups, the Mosque Committee and the Association for the Revival of the Heritage of 'Ayn el-Mreisse, stood up for the fishermen and exchanged their votes in the 1996 parliamentary elections for promises to find an alternative fishing port. Indeed, this alliance prompted a parliament member to intervene, and as a result, the municipality offered to build an alternative fishing port away from the al-Aḥlam building. The new port, located in the vicinity of the Ḥammam al-Askari area, a relatively faraway location, was to retain the name ʿAyn el-Mreisse Fishing Port and would serve all the fishermen of Beirut. The fishermen of ʿAyn el-Mreisse refused the proposed solution. They argued that the port wouldn't be big enough for all the fishermen and that the proposed area was not suitable for fishing, since its location in an area exposed to heavy currents would not offer protection for their boats.

Although the fishermen's attempts to preserve the fishing port did not stop the construction of the al-Aḥlam building, the port became a site of nostalgia for many Beirutis, including some who lived outside the neighborhood. Local artists produced several paintings that portrayed the port and the fishermen as they were in the past. A painter named George, who lived in the neighborhood, became part of Abu ʿAdnan's circle and showed me his paintings of the fishing port. One of them was of the Mediterranean at sunset. The oil painting portrayed the gray rocks that rested peacefully in the calm water while two green fishing boats sailed on the surface of the sea. However, it is interesting that Corniche Street and the buildings facing the port were not visible in George's painting. According to George, ʿAyn el-Mreisse and its fishing port were the only remaining markers of Old Beirut (Beirut Zamman). George felt that it was his responsibility to document this part of the city's heritage for future generations. Similar to the fishermen, George looked to the sea and ignored the land. All of them shared the feeling that the new buildings erected by developers had destroyed their neighborhood.

Unlike the fishermen and the local artists who campaigned to preserve the neighborhood and protect it from the newly constructed buildings, Future TV (owned by Hariri) used the image of the same fishing port to promote the prime minister's agendas of construction and modernity. The station ran a video clip with a moving image of young, happy fishermen in their boats sailing in the shadow of high-rise buildings while a local singer sang "The country is moving, the work is going forward, you don't need to worry" (*El-balad mashi wa el shighil mashi, wlaa yhimak*). According to this promotional video clip, the new structures were viewed positively and it was assumed that all Beirutis, including the fishermen, were content about the outcome.

Although the majority of the neighborhood's residents believed that the fishermen had the right to the port, they expected that the fishermen would lose their battle against the powerful developers of the al-Aḥlam building who were supported by the government and the prime minister. It was even rumored that Hariri's son and relatives of other high-ranking officials had bought apartments in that building.

"WHOSE LIGHTS WILL STAY ON?": THE MOSQUE COMMITTEE

Similar to the fishermen who lost their port to developers, the Mosque Committee of ʿAyn el-Mreisse tackled another global player, in this case, the Hard Rock Cafe. The Mosque Committee, established in the 1960s, was one of the oldest local community-based organizations in the neighborhood. Its members were mostly Sunni Muslims who considered themselves among the original residents of the area. The committee provided services to area residents both before and during the war. Members claimed that before the war, they sponsored students to attend college and assisted needy families; during the war, they ran schools, collected aid for displaced families, coordinated with political authorities to provide water and electricity to local residents, and maintained stability in the area by reducing the tensions between the combating militias. However, in the aftermath of the war, the Mosque Committee faced new challenges. Among them was finding ways to negotiate with the increasing number of developers and businesses moving into the neighborhood.

When the Hard Rock Cafe announced plans to open directly across the street from the mosque, the committee tried to prevent it. Members of the committee invoked a city law that compels entertainment establishments that play loud music and serve alcohol to keep a distance of at least fifty meters from any religious establishment. The committee's appeals failed when city officials included the width of the curb in measuring the distance between the mosque and the Hard Rock Cafe. The committee members accused the owner of using his business connections to influence city officials. In December of 1997, the Hard Rock Cafe opened with a gala event attended by numerous investors and dignitaries, including Prime Minister Rafik Hariri himself. Each night from then on, the Hard Rock Cafe's loud Western music competed with the mosque's call to prayer.

Despite its location in the heart of ʿAyn el-Mreisse, local residents did not patronize the Hard Rock Cafe, nor did it become part of their everyday vocabulary. In fact, it remained a metaphorically invisible site despite its shining neon sign and the giant red glass guitar placed at its entrance. Interestingly, when area inhabitants gave directions, they often referred to an army checkpoint located next to the Hard Rock Cafe instead of using the latter as a landmark. Residents felt alienated from these new international establishments. As Hassan, an 'Ayn el-Mreisse resident, explained: "These foreign businesses are not built for us [the local residents]; they are for the rich and the tourists." Only a few of the area's residents with whom I spoke had ever visited the Hard Rock Cafe. Shadi, one of the few who had, described his visit:

> Two weeks after the opening, I went there with my friend Ahmad. We dressed like the customers of the cafe so the guard at the door wouldn't stop us. Immediately after we sat down, a waitress who was wearing a skirt this long [pointing to five inches above his knee], came to take our order. She spoke to us in English. To aggravate her, I said in Arabic: "Give me a Bloody Mary without alcohol!" The waitress condescendingly repeated in English, "You want two orders of Bloody Mary." The waitress did not come back to us, but a waiter brought us the drinks. We sat there for fifteen minutes and left.

The Hard Rock Cafe was among the first restaurants and bars to employ waitresses. Shadi and his friend Ahmad were shocked to see a Lebanese waitress serving alcohol. Although it was quite evident that Shadi's animosity toward the Cafe predated his visit, his experience there did little to change his opinion.

When I asked the Cafe's manager, a Lebanese-American from Ohio, why they chose this specific location, he explained that his choice was based on the recommendations of an international consulting firm that conducted the feasibility study. He also admitted he did not have any knowledge of the area and its residents, nor did he express any interest in acquiring any. According to him, the Cafe had nothing to do with the residents of the area because its customers were mainly rich young Lebanese, foreigners who lived in Beirut, and tourists.

While the Mosque Committee's plea to stop the opening of the Hard Rock Cafe was based on moral grounds, other residents complained that the Cafe did not bring any economic gains to their area. When compared to prewar entertainment establishments, the Hard Rock Cafe was often criticized for not contributing to the local economy. Salim, a member of the Mosque Committee who had lived in the area all of his life, compared the Saint Georges, a prewar luxury hotel and yacht club, to the Hard Rock Cafe as follows:

The enormous guitar marking the new Hard Rock Cafe at the base of a new building. The mosque faces the sign.

Cityscape on the border of 'Ayn el-Mreisse in 1997. The edifice behind the palm trees was the prewar world-class Saint Georges Hotel, where former prime minister Hariri was later assassinated in 2005. The building in the center is a prewar hotel that was later occupied by the war-displaced.

The majority of the waiters and workers at the Saint Georges lived here. The managers knew the grocer, the butcher, and all shopkeepers in the area. They bought the hotel's vegetables and meat from us. When the employees of the Saint Georges walked in the streets, they used to say "Good morning" and "How are you," unlike [the employees of] the Hard Rock Cafe. All we've gained [from the Hard Rock Cafe] is the noise [of the music and the honking cars] and the heavy traffic. As you can see, the streets are blocked all night by the cars of the Cafe's rich customers!

It is important to note here that the objection to the Hard Rock Cafe by the Mosque Committee and to the al-Aḥlam building by the fishermen was not due to their foreignness or global character. On the contrary, neighborhood residents were familiar with the potential benefits of international investments and remembered with nostalgia their interaction with the workers of prewar cosmopolitan establishments. Rather, they objected to the lack of effort on the part of the new businesses to involve area residents in their plans. For example, they distrusted the presence of the Hard Rock Cafe because they felt it was a place to which they were denied access.

The presence of global institutions and outsiders was not entirely new. In fact, 'Ayn el-Mreisse was a premier prewar tourist destination known for its luxury hotels (the Saint Georges, the Phoenicia, and the Holiday Inn), its nightclubs of the red-light district on Martínez Street, and its furnished apartments. When they recalled the history of their neighborhood, residents often listed the names of the international hotels and the names of well-known world politicians and personalities who stayed at these hotels. Some of the people I interviewed insisted on showing me photos they had taken of movie stars, world leaders, and Western tourists. Additionally, residents typically offered up a list of foreign embassies that had residences in 'Ayn el-Mreisse (American, Austrian, French, German, and British) and emphasized that they maintained good relationships with embassy officials. Abu Ḥussam, a fisherman and a retired boxer who had lived in the same house for over sixty years, described his relationship to a high-ranking official at the French Embassy, which one could interpret as having a colonial/sexual nexus:

> When I was young, I was a strong athlete [showing me his arm muscles]. Once, I was swimming with my friends around here, and a secretary in the French Embassy noticed me. He sent his Lebanese driver to invite me for a coffee. When he learned that I am also a boxing champion, he hired me to exercise with him for three hours every day. . . . He used to pay me five liras . . . that was good money. Later on, I started to give his wife massages.

Abu Ḥussam compared his interactions with the official at the French Embassy to the alienation he felt as a result of the dramatic changes in his neighborhood. He also regretted the lack of social exchange and the loss of economic opportunities. He continued:

> Now, there is an attack on 'Ayn el-Mreisse by the Hariri men, the investors and the developers. They already confiscated the beaches in the area to pave the highway that connects the airport to the Solidere area [downtown Beirut]. These beaches used to attract both foreign and Arab tourists as well as Lebanese. Also, these beaches were a source of livelihood for us. Each beach employed ten to fifteen men.

As this quote indicates, the residents of 'Ayn el-Mreisse celebrated the neighborhood's cosmopolitan past but condemned the postwar global initiatives because they viewed them as antagonistic to the local economic and social fabric.

Although they failed to prevent the opening of the Hard Rock Cafe, the Mosque Committee played a strong role by starting a number of initiatives to preserve the neighborhood's endangered past. The committee recruited young members, who then contacted municipal agencies and politicians to facilitate the establishment of a public library. Although the municipality accepted the application, the library did not open. In an effort to protect the area from the influx of new businesses, the committee sought Sunni investors as commercial partners to discourage members from selling their property to outsiders. In addition, committee members mediated emerging conflicts. For example, a respected elder, who is a committee member, would place social and moral pressure on a landlord to renew a lease agreement for a long-standing poor tenant. The Mosque Committee is an example of a local group that was afraid that the dramatic postwar spatial changes would result in the destruction of the community's social fabric.

THE ASSOCIATION FOR THE REVIVAL OF THE HERITAGE OF ʿAYN EL-MREISSE

Another active community group in ʿAyn el-Mreisse was the Association for the Revival of the Heritage of ʿAyn el-Mreisse.[3] It was an example of another collective action taken by marginalized locals, who organized themselves to preserve the heritage of their neighborhood as they saw it and to record the memories of its original residents in a local museum. Members of this association came primarily from three ethnoreligious groups, Druze, Sunni, and Christian, who all viewed themselves among the original residents of the neighborhood.

The association's understanding of the concept of "heritage" was a flexible one. Najem, a middle-aged retired fireman who also worked as a fisherman and a diver before he lost both of his legs in an explosion, had transformed his own house into what he called the "Museum of ʿAyn el-Mreisse." Residents of the neighborhood acknowledged the leadership of Najem and referred to him as "the one who can tell the history of the neighborhood," and they donated things they no longer used but judged as valuable to his collection. Najem described the association's objective as "the preservation of anything old, authentic, and used by the people of ʿAyn el-Mreisse." This flexible definition of heritage, and the extent of his neighbors' cooperation, was manifested in the jammed three-room

One display case in the Museum of ʿAyn el-Mreisse

Wall display of photos of Old Beirut at the Museum of ʿAyn el-Mreisse

museum that held, among other things, forty albums of old photographs; a collection of old radio sets, telephones, and phonographs; traditional Beiruti clothes; coins from different parts of the world; paintings and postcards of Old Beirut; and hundreds of seashells collected from the shores surrounding Beirut.

Najem emphasized the importance of his museum as a way to guarantee the continued existence of the area. Najem saw himself as a guardian of the neighborhood's threatened past and the memories of its residents. He was convinced that his museum was vital to protecting the past not only of the neighborhood but also of the whole city. He explained that

'Ayn el-Mreisse is what is left of Old Beirut, which is also on its way to disappearing. If you come back to this area in ten years, I am sure that you won't find any of us here, and you won't recognize the area. I am trying to protect the past of the area and the memory of its residents. I believe that our heritage is our history and our existence.

Although Najem did not have a systematic method for organizing the museum material, he did have an elaborate knowledge of his collection, such as the names of the items, the names of owners and donors, the approximate year they were originally purchased, the prices the original owners paid for selected items, and, most interestingly, an anecdote about most of the items. For example, Najem enthusiastically recounted the story of an old radio set: "This was the first radio set in 'Ayn el-Mreisse. The owner, who was a carpenter and a friend of my father, had sold his workshop equipment to purchase this radio in the 1930s. Every night, the neighbors went to the carpenter's shop to listen to the radio." Najem told similar stories about other items in his collection. Each of these items was connected to a story that was embedded in the social network of the neighborhood's residents. Although this knowledge was not written anywhere, it was reproduced orally; and it was perpetuated in the collective memories and the shared knowledge of Najem and his friends, reflected mainly in the stories they shared about the museum's collection.

As the inventory of phonographs and telephones suggested, Najem's collection was not limited to items manufactured or made locally. The museum included anything adopted or owned by the residents of the neighborhood over time, regardless of the item's origin. In fact, many of the items in the collection, like the telephones, represented moments of *modernity*, and not authenticity,[4] especially at the time when they were first used by the neighborhood's inhabitants. Najem's story of the carpenter's radio was an example of this irony. According to Najem, if an item was used by the inhabitants of ʿAyn el-Mreisse in the past, it became part of the heritage and deserved preservation, whether it be an appliance, coins, clothing, or fishing equipment.

One of the complex examples of objects in Najem's museum that come from "outside" the neighborhood was the collection of photographs. The collection included photographs of international celebrities, such as Hollywood actors and actresses, the Shah of Iran, (the late) King Hussein of Jordan, the American boxer Muhammad Ali, and employees of different embassies whom Najem knew by name—portraits taken when the person was visiting the neighborhood as a tourist. For Najem and his constituency, these photos illustrated a crucial aspect of ʿAyn el-Mreisse's heritage, namely, that the neighborhood's beaches, nightclubs, and hotels had attracted many foreign visitors, some of whom had formed temporary friendships with local residents. Najem and his friends expressed pride in the neighborhood's past when it was a site of attraction for outsiders and tourists, but at the same time, they complained about the postwar version of tourism, a commodification of the neighborhood's natural environment and what they described as "the invasion of strangers who did not belong to the area." Abu ʿAdnan, another member of the association, disparaged these strangers by saying: "With their money, they can buy apartments with beautiful views of the sea, but, alas, they do not know their actual meaning. They only watch the sea through the glass of their air-conditioned balconies." Other members of the association criticized the newcomers for not appreciating the unique character of the neighborhood and its "authentic" past and for not interacting with the original residents. Through the museum's displays, Najem and members of his association aspired to document and preserve certain moments of the past as a way of providing the area with roots in the present.

In addition to housing and displaying the items that were believed to represent ʿAyn el-Mreisse's past, the museum functioned as a site of remembrance for the neighborhood's residents. Sitting in a big armchair under a vine tree on the balcony of his old house, overlooking an alleyway and accompanied with other co-founders, his aging mother, and two sisters, Najem narrated what could be called the "biographies" of his collection. During these narrations, his friends and family members complemented his story by interjecting more details, making comments, or prompting Najem to show his guests the new items he had just acquired. It was apparent that Najem's friends had heard the same stories before, but they continued to seem interested in listening to them again. His family as well as other members of his association became active participants in telling the story of their neighborhood's past through talking about the museum's collection. They seemed to perceive the "biographies" of the museum collection as an extension of their own lives.

The museum/home exuded the quality of a social center, where familiar friends banter and strangers (like myself) were welcomed as an audience. One of Najem's colleagues was Abu 'Adnan, the cheerful, talkative eighty-year-old retired fisherman and butcher. He spent most of his time sitting with Najem on his balcony, watching the passersby. Abu 'Adnan had given Najem an assortment of intimate and personal items that became part of the museum's collection: photographs, an old butcher scale and meat hooks that he once used in his shop, his father's traditional Beiruti dress and traditional wooden sandals. He also contributed personal stories associated with each item. One afternoon, Abu 'Adnan asked Najem to show me his father's traditional Beiruti robes, and when Najem obliged, Abu 'Adnan recounted a story from his boyhood. He told the story of the day he followed his father in the old alleys of Beirut and got lost. When he started crying, a shopkeeper recognized him and took him back to his family's house. A third member of the association teased Abu 'Adnan by saying that he had given the items to the museum because his wife wanted them out of their house. Abu 'Adnan jokingly replied that he had given them to the museum so he could gain the right to keep telling stories about his own life. While Abu 'Adnan talked about his memories of his father, George, the neighborhood painter, jumped into the conversation and told us about his grandfather, who used to wear the same traditional Beiruti garb. Three of George's original paintings depicting twilight in the neighborhood's fishing port were hanging on a crowded main wall in the museum.

Like Abu 'Adnan's donations, the rest of the museum's collection consisted of familiar but no-longer-used items. The items became symbols in the interrelated processes of collective remembering and the preservation of the neighborhood's past. The 'Ayn el-Mreisse museum served multiple purposes: it was a kind of archive, a site of memory for the residents of the neighborhood who were keen on sorting and preserving their memories, one that offered the possibility of teaching others (like me) about the lost past; and it was a place for socializing, where members of the community discussed their concerns, argued their political positions on important issues related to their lives, and engaged in dialogue that reinforced their affiliations.

In addition to operating the neighborhood's museum, the Association for the Revival of the Heritage of 'Ayn el-Mreisse supported the fishermen in their struggle against investors and developers. The organization's solidarity with the fishermen's cause was manifested when members of the association, along with members of the Mosque Committee, coordinated their votes in the parliamentary elections to support candidates who promised to defend the fishermen. As explained by members of the association, the support of the fishermen was seen as one way of protecting an important aspect of the neighborhood's threatened heritage. Although the neighborhood museum was primarily run by Najem, it was the efforts and the passion of his neighbors that made the museum a site of collective memory.

The phenomena that I have been describing are reminiscent of Andreas Huyssen's comment that memory has become a "cultural obsession." Huyssen explains the political reasons that make communities preserve their collective memories by creating public spheres of real memory. These sites counter the politics of forgetting imposed by ruling regimes either through reconciliation or through repressive silencing. "In sum, memory has become a cultural obsession of monumental proportions across the globe" (Huyssen 2000, 26).

"WE PERFORMED THERE, TOO": THE BEIRUT THEATER

Another site used to restore cultural memory was the Beirut Theater. In 1993, a group of artists and intellectuals took it upon themselves to renovate the Beirut Theater, the oldest theater in the city. Using private and corporate funds, membership contributions, and the sale of tickets, the theater staged local, regional, and international performances; exhibited art shows; and hosted conferences until it was forced to close down in 2001 because of financial difficulties.

The theater was built in the early 1950s as a movie house that was named the Hilton Cinema. Later on, in 1965, the owner, a French-educated Lebanese entrepreneur, and his French theater director had changed the cinema into a playhouse where Western plays and musicals were staged for the city's educated cosmopolitan elite. In the 1970s, because of the war and the escalation of violence, most cultural and entertainment activities were suspended. At this point, the theater served another function. The successive political parties and militias used it as a "war theater." The Progressive Socialist Party, the Murabitoun, Hizballah, and the Amal Movement each controlled the theater at various times. There they celebrated victories, memorialized martyrs, delivered political speeches, commemorated religious ceremonies, and even stored weapons. Neighborhood residents I spoke to passionately remembered the theater during the war. Munir, a member of the Progressive Socialist Party, stated that "the site became a theater of our operations (*masrraḥ li 'amalyatna*). There, we paid tribute to our martyrs, held oratorical festivals for hundreds of supporters, broadcast radio news, and used the basement as a shelter." Later on, the Shi'ite political party, Amal Movement, used the theater for similar purposes as they commemorated the ten holy days of the 'Ashura' ritual, a significant Shi'ite religious ceremony. For the majority of the spectators who attended the events of the Amal Movement, namely, displaced peasants and women, it was their first time to enter a theater building.

Paradoxically, when it ceased its role as a "war theater" and started to stage plays and films once again, the Beirut Theater became off-limits for those who had taken part in its wartime functions. Huda, the theater's new director, recalled a conversation with a Shi'ite woman who lived in the neighborhood. She told me that in 1994, a few months after the official reopening of the theater, a woman stopped her and said, "I feel so sorry every time I pass by this place. For many years we celebrated 'Ashura' here. It used to be a sanctified place (*makan ṭaher*), but, alas, look at it now! They changed it into a playhouse." When Huda told the woman that in fact she worked there, the woman suspiciously asked, "What kind of work do you do inside? Do you dance naked in front of men?" To which Huda replied, not wishing to offend the woman: "No, God forbid, I am just a secretary here; anyway, we do not do that kind of dance." Huda was quite surprised when the woman asked her for a job for her recently divorced daughter. The director expressed some uncertainty as to how the theater would be received by the locals. Huda then told me that although she herself had lived in 'Ayn el-Mreisse before the war, she felt that she was not familiar with the neighbors. In fact, she chose to disassociate herself from the residents because of their economic and social status.

The local residents watched the renovations with suspicion. Some viewed the theater as yet another project designed to serve the elite. Unlike the Hard Rock Cafe and the Dreams Building, where the locals did not feel welcome, some residents did venture into the theater building and occasionally attended some functions, such as a photo exhibit about the Israeli occupation of South Lebanon.

At the theater, I attended Lebanese plays in which the war was the main plot, Arabic plays from Morocco and Tunisia, an Iranian film festival, the Czech Ballet, and a conference that honored the life and work of Edward Said. Paul, a writer and a co-manager at the theater, explained the rea-

A temporary booth used to perform the Shi'ite 'Ashura' ritual

sons that prevented the neighbors from frequenting the place by saying: "When they [poor locals] want entertainment, they look for something faraway from their familiar surroundings."

Although the theater managed to attract a wide range of audiences, like many other not-for-profit postwar venues, it faced serious financial problems. The government was blamed for its inadequate support for the arts, and the city's new elite, for their poor artistic taste. The director shared this opinion and criticized the Beirutis for not appreciating good art. For example, when the theater exhibited the work of renowned artists whose work was sold at major galleries in Cairo and Paris, the viewers did not express interest in buying these works. But when they showed the work of a local artist who belonged to a large "clan," all of his work was bought by members of his extended family. The theater director commented about such an artist: "His work was pretty decent; he painted realistic scenes from his village, and his relatives paid for the work because they knew him and were able to recognize this hill or that house. What can I tell you? It is the tribal mentality." The director expressed frustration about the lack of appreciation for fine art.

Rana, a supporter and a member of the theater, blamed the postwar nouveaux riches for not supporting high art. She sarcastically described the uninterested postwar elite as "warlords who made their money from the sale of weapons. They do not care about the arts. They'd rather display their wealth by going to fancy restaurants or buying expensive cars. They don't see plays or donate money to support the arts." Along the same lines, Etel Adnan, a novelist and journalist, presented a grim picture of the conditions of the arts in postwar Beirut because "money became the new lord." Adnan expressed concern about the survival of the city's two main theaters, the Beirut Theater and Al-Madina Theater:

> They [the theaters] did and do interesting work, but support for them, instead of growing, is dwindling, and they may close for lack of money. When one thinks that some rich people give parties which run into a million dollars just to satisfy some inflated ego and do not give a penny for a cultural creation, one is heart-broken indeed. (Adnan 1998a, 4)

In addition to the lack of funding from the government and the uninterested elite, some attributed the financial difficulties to the location of the theater, which did not appeal to the bourgeoisie. Paul, who was present at the time of the interview with Huda, added:

> When we reopened the theater, people thought we were crazy, and some bet that we would not survive for more than six months. A banker who lived in East Beirut asked me, "How is the area these days? Do you think we can come down there now?" Many wished the theater was located somewhere else. For the bourgeoisie, the area is not up to their standards; they still see it as a run-down area (*msharshaḥá*).

After six years of struggle, the Beirut Theater closed down. Although it was remembered and mourned by its supporters, it did not survive the postwar challenges.

CONCLUDING REMARKS

Relying on their collective past and shared spatial memories, the less powerful residents of 'Ayn el-Mreisse defied their exclusion from the newly built spaces by creating long-term alliances, and, sometimes, by forming nongovernmental organizations to claim public sites. Although each collective employed different tactics to claim different spaces, all four neighborhood public spaces—a fishing port, a mosque, a museum, and a theater—shared the quality of becoming a site of collective remembrance and nostalgia. All the advocates invoked their past relationships to specific spaces in their struggles. Each group also combined other tactics besides memory to confront the conditions of uncertainty and the intrusive transformation in their area. The fishermen who fought to preserve their presence at the port instead of the luxury apartment building invoked their continuous presence in the port for hundreds of years and their extensive knowledge of the sea; besides memory, they called on religion by claiming that the "sea is God's property."

Similarly, the Mosque Committee recalled its long history of service in the area, and for a more practical tactic, it pointed to a municipal law in its efforts to obstruct the opening of the Hard Rock Cafe. The Association for the Revival of the Heritage of 'Ayn el-Mreisse decided to counter the erasure of the physical buildings not only by discourse, but by physically establishing a museum commemorating the neighborhood's past. Finally, the Beirut Theater collective recounted its prewar experiences of running the same theater prior to the war; unlike the other groups, it did not combine different tactics, but it also summoned its inherent enhancement to the area as an educated cultural producer.

The next chapter moves beyond 'Ayn el-Mreisse and shifts to another kind of public site, coffee-drinking venues, and the different responses to postwar uncertainty they presented.

This chapter examines the relationships of Beirutis to specific urban public spaces and the sense of place they provided before, during, and after
the war. In particular, it analyzes the ways the social understanding of time
and place is expressed through memory at a time when competition over
space reached its height in the unpredictable postwar environment. As I
look at issues involving space and memory, I examine postwar "temporality" by analyzing specific coffee-drinking venues. Based on interviews
with men, women, academics, artists, and ordinary residents, the chapter
presents the ways specific public sites are remembered and recalled.

The following cases of remembering and forgetting explore some of
the differences and intersections between gendered groups in their recollections of public spaces before and during the war. The spaces in question were not official political arenas, nor were they former battlegrounds,
but rather were ordinary spaces, ones where Beirutis gathered around the
practice of drinking coffee.

Coffee-drinking venues in Beirut provide case studies of some of
Lebanon's very real and complex postwar dilemmas. By examining the
recollected narratives centered on the experiences of socializing and
drinking coffee at prewar French-style cafés, wartime funeral homes, and
postwar expresso vans, the chapter presents the ways in which gender,
class, and temporality are linked to prohibited and accessible spaces.

RECALLING PREWAR TIMES AND SPACES

In the reconstruction era, prewar Beirut had become a historical utopia.
As mentioned earlier, one finds it described as having been the cosmopolitan center of the Middle East, the "East's window to the West," and
"the Paris of the Arab world." Authors often praised the prewar city as
a place that enabled an international community to feel very much at
home, and as a place that functioned as a regional center for finance,

commerce, and other economic activities for the entire Middle East. In addition to its crucial economic role, Beirut was remembered through oral and written accounts as a place where men and women, intellectuals, artists, and writers exchanged ideas and engaged in intellectual debate. In an interview I conducted with Niqola Ziadeh, a retired history professor, he praised his favorite city as unique: "Beirut is different from both Damascus and Amman. A French person can easily live in Beirut, but not in Damascus or Amman." Ziadeh had lived in a number of cities in Palestine, Jordan, Syria, England, and the United States, but he nonetheless had felt homeless, stateless, and jobless. He said, "As a Palestinian, Beirut rescued me." During the 1950s and 1960s, he recalled that there were, on average, 2.5 cultural activities (concerts, lectures, workshops) per day in the area of Ras Beirut that housed the American University, the Spanish Cultural Center, and the Italian Institute, as well as other local cultural organizations.

The Lebanese remembered and documented prewar and wartime periods through various means: they created art, including theater plays, visual work, and film; published memoirs, historical accounts, and coffee-table books of photographs;[1] and founded museums, both on the official and unofficial levels. They also launched Internet Web sites where individuals posted memories, old photos, or notices seeking lost friends and family members. The authors of these works believed that healing the wounds of the war and preventing a future civil war could be accomplished only by confronting the past, especially the brutality of the war.

Prewar and wartime memories are gendered. Men and women recalled different sites as accessible or prohibited. In their recollections of their prewar experiences, educated Beiruti women nostalgically described a sophisticated, vibrant urban setting. They emphasized their experiences of crossing social, familial, and religious borders in their attempts to set up places for themselves in public life. In an interview with me, Ilham, a professor at a local university, described the situation of women in the 1960s: "At that time, women were visible in almost all public spaces without necessarily being accompanied or guarded by men." In Ilham's case, many of the places that were prohibited for her mother's generation became accessible to her.

Before the sixties, women's spatial movement was restricted to traditional spaces such as the hairdresser, the tailor, houses of close relatives, and some local shops. At that time, only a handful of women worked outside their homes.

In recalling social sites for middle-class women, Ilham did not acknowledge that these "proper women" continued to be prohibited from a number of sites considered "public spaces," for example, the red-light district, which at night was used exclusively by men and female sex workers, or the exclusively traditional male spaces such as the traditional coffeehouses.

THE DICHOTOMY OF PUBLIC AND PRIVATE SPACE

Through describing and analyzing the memories and experiences of men and women about specific coffee-drinking venues in Beirut, this chapter questions the "public/private" dichotomy that dominates the ethnographic writings about Arab and Middle Eastern societies. The notions of public and private domains continue to be central themes in anthropological literature. Many writings demonstrate the complexity of using the concepts of private/public domains and show the ways their meanings have changed over time. Generally speaking, public space meant the open, the accessible, and the communal, while private space referred to the domestic, the confined, and the personal. Feminist philosophers Seyla Benhabib and Nancy Fraser questioned this dichotomy and called for the complexification rather than the simplification of the private and the public, both theoretically and practically (Benhabib 1997; Fraser 1992). Despite such calls for questioning, literature on the public and the private in the Arab world continues to utilize the binary oppositions of outside/inside, political/domestic, and public/private as acceptable paradigms for analyzing these communities as segregated worlds of males and females. This outlook is reflected in statements such as "Women may only exist in the private domain in socially closed spaces. They have no public and open life" (Gilsenan 1982, 172).

In his 1999 textbook about the Middle East and Central Asia, Dale Eickelman supported the assumption of the existence of two separate worlds for men and women and cited a number of studies that affirmed such stereotypes (Eickelman 1998, 182–183). Similarly, Pierre Bourdieu linked the architecture of the traditional Algerian Kabyle house, the practical functions associated with each of its sections, and its cultural connotations with dualistic categories of male/female, house/market, day/night, upper/lower, and right/left. He concluded that the Kabyle house was a microcosm of the "same oppositions that governed the universe" (Bourdieu 1979, 128). Although the book was originally published in 1972, it continues to be cited for its factual data.

These writings describe Arab communities as worlds divided into male/

female and public/private spheres in which men were viewed as dominant, powerful, political, and in control of the public sphere, while women were viewed as subordinate, nonpolitical, and confined to the domestic space. However, a number of women writers highlighted women's implicit and indirect role in influencing the "public" and the political (Abu-Lughod 1989; Roxann 1976). These studies trace the changes in women's roles and focus on the "informal" roles of women, who, within their extended family, engage in politics as fully as men but in a discreet way not open to public scrutiny.[2]

The following narratives of coffee-drinking sites in Beirut demonstrate that the binaries of public/private and men/women were inadequate to fully analyze the social meaning of gendered public spaces in Beirut. The ethnographic data in this chapter present the diverse intersection of accessible and prohibited spaces, and the construction of space, time, and identities in public arenas. In Beirut, European-style prewar cafés were viewed as modern public spaces because they hosted different cultural and social activities and were open to all. They were remembered as sites where Beirutis from different religious backgrounds were able to meet and mingle. Moreover, the cafés were described as "public" places where men and women socialized together away from the privacy of their homes. As public places, however, they were, in fact, accessible only to the intellectuals who could afford them and to those who felt comfortable crossing social, gender, and religious boundaries. Hence, these cafés were "prohibited" locations for those who could not cross these lines because of either financial or social limitations. Working-class Beirutis had different prewar coffee-drinking experiences. In the social geography of coffee drinking, working-class men took their coffee in traditional,[3] not French-style, cafés, while working-class women drank coffee at home.

CAFÉS AS PREWAR SITES OF SOCIALIZING

When I started my fieldwork, the café scene in Beirut was not one of my central concerns. When arranging interviews, many of my women subjects suggested that we meet at the famous Modca Café located on Hamra Street, one of the few surviving prewar European-style cafés.[4] During the interview, the café where we sat conjured up memories related to other prewar cafés. It was striking how often cafés were discussed and how passionately they were remembered. Subsequently, I began to ask my interviewees about their prewar and wartime memories of coffee drinking.

When middle-class intellectuals and writers remembered prewar Beirut, what they romanticized and recalled with "nostalgia" and longing was the Hamra Street scene.[5] During the 1950s–1960s, as Beirut became the main financial and cultural center of the region,[6] a number of what were known as "modern cafés" opened on Hamra Street in the Ras Beirut area. The street was a commercial and residential area for the upper and middle classes. Zeina, the director of a nongovernmental organization for the empowerment of women, described Hamra Street as "a place where women walked freely. It was a place for women to celebrate fashion and modernity. [She snorted.] It was believed then that in order to demonstrate that you were a liberated woman you had to look European. . . . I mean *French*." The street housed cafés with names such as the Horseshoe, the Dolce Vita, the Modca, the Wimpy, and the Express. The names themselves illustrated the desire to embody a cosmopolitan identity. These cafés were remembered as places where Beirut's intelligentsia, both women and men, engaged in intellectual and political debates while they consumed Western beverages such as espresso, instant coffee, and tea made from tea bags, along with Western desserts, rather than the local beverages and snacks served in the *maqha*, the traditional coffeehouse. Interestingly, the only item that appeared on both menus was the "Arabic or Turkish" coffee. Amina, a painter and a poet, colorfully described these cafés as "places for breathing freedom, and as sites frequented by women on a daily basis."

Each social group adopted a particular café, and each café gained a unique reputation. For example, the Horseshoe was frequented by intellectuals, poets, writers, and artists. The women who attended this café, as one of them explained, "[had] already crossed the border of worrying about their reputation, the fear that people will talk negatively about them." Those who patronized these cafés described themselves as "liberated women" (*nisa' mutaharirat*) who were willing to take complete responsibility for their behavior.

A group of acquaintances usually clustered at a particular table or in the corner of a café, which gave the meeting a resemblance to an intimate gathering at home. Mona, an artist, described her relationship to one table at the Horseshoe Café: "At one point, I felt that that small old table became an extension of my own living room." Mona's memories also marked her personal history in the café: "In that spot, we discussed each other's work (writings and paintings), fought over political issues, read newspapers, wrote letters, borrowed each other's books, made new friends and lovers, and lost others. If the walls or chairs could ever speak, they would be the best ones to tell our stories." Mona articulated what all my interviewees seemed to feel—that their histories were contained in the places they gathered for coffee. Similarly, in his book about social and entertainment places in Beirut, Amjad Nasir (1996) revealed that many poems, books, and political statements were drafted in Hamra Street cafés. Firyal, another interviewee, explained the social atmosphere of the café: "If I wanted to get in touch with some of my friends, I knew where to find them, either I went to the Horseshoe or to the Dolce Vita. If they were not there, I would leave them a note at the café."

Although some of the customers did not know each other person-ally, they usually knew each other's work and seemed to share a common worldview. Ilham explained the requirements for frequenting one specific café: "In order to become part of the scene at the Horseshoe, one had to get involved in the discourse of its customers (*badik tudkhuli ila khitabu-hum*), that is, one had to more or less speak the same language, politically or otherwise."

Other cafés were also known as gathering sites for groups who shared specific social and political ideologies. Beirutis I interviewed and writ-ings on the topic described the Dolce Vita as a place where Arab political opposition debated revolutionary and political beliefs. Political activist and writer Amjad Nasir states that the plans for revolutions and major po-litical changes in neighboring countries took place at the cafés of Hamra Street (1996). Ironically, the presence of the revolutionary figures and the political opposition attracted secret agents and spies of Arab and foreign regimes, which made the majority of the crowd at the Dolce Vita men.

Prior to the war, Arab businessmen frequented the Modca Café, but when most of the Hamra Street cafés closed during the war, the intellec-tuals migrated there, and thus the presence of women increased dramati-cally. The Express Café, located across the street from the daily newspaper *Annahar*, opened later and functioned as a meeting place for journalists and writers. It offered a more upper-class atmosphere and was mostly frequented by women.

For women such as Ilham, Firyal, and Mona, the café scene was re-membered as a collective intimate space. Women viewed access to the cafés as empowering and a sign of being modern. When they attended these European-style places, they were able to step outside what some of them described as the traditional patrilinial hierarchies. Here I would argue that the café offered a certain kind of freedom, precisely because it was a liminal space for both men and women, located outside the usual sphere of gift giving and other social obligations. It was a public space, exposed to the gaze of outsiders, and it was frequented by men *and* women yet still respectable and socially acceptable. Each café was an intimate space for those who frequented the same café on a regular basis and who sat mostly at the same table each time. Maha summarized the advantages of going there:

> It was easy to meet someone at a café. This was not deemed a formal meeting or a date. It was different from inviting people over to your house or visiting people's homes: you did not need to serve as a host or take a present. At the café, you were liberated from time constraints. You could choose to leave or stay at any time.

This freedom enabled relationships beyond the traditional networks dictated by marriage and kin. Both women and men described cafés as places where one could bring together an alternative "family" of friends with whom one shared beliefs and political worldviews. The café was also remembered as a haven from heat, humidity, and the congested traffic of the city. In 2003, the *Annahar* daily newspaper memorialized the closure of the Modca, the last surviving prewar Hamra Street café. In this article, the author mourned the loss of the Modca and recalled the time he had spent there on a hot, humid summer day:

> An extremely hot and sticky day usually ended with an invitation from the glass windows of the Modca. That was a call to go inside to an air-conditioned womb where safety, comfort, and refreshments were found. . . . The passersby searched for temptation and found it at the café. Then, they themselves became objects of temptation when they were inside. Although you were an observer, when you sat next to the glass windows, you became the subject of the gazes of those who sat inside and those who walked outside. (*Annahar,* September 4, 2003)

Those who attended the Hamra Street modern cafés spoke with a great deal of sentiment about the availability of shops and cafés that "happily offered their contents" to the passing pedestrians. This revisiting of the past was connected to the present, a time when middle-class women lost access to familiar venues for socializing and intellectual debate. The lack of social space represented a state of uncertainty, loss, and feeling like a foreigner in one's own surroundings that the war and its aftermath had created. Interviewees believed that the new buildings were designed to alienate rather than make them feel welcome. They also remarked on the lack of a sense of belonging in the new spaces. One woman said that "the glass walls—now—are similar to the air bags in a car: its function starts only when the car is not usable anymore."

When the war ended, the owner of the Horseshoe Café started a new café named the City Café in the hope of re-creating the atmosphere of the old Horseshoe. However, the new place failed. One of the old customers described the new City Café as inauthentic: "They have a nicer design and furniture, but those who can afford the City Café are incapable of bringing back the old atmosphere."

Reactions to the new forms of coffee venues vary. Ilham viewed the return of the modern café to Beirut as a healthy phenomenon for women because it gives them the chance to become part of the public scene. She believed that the absence of the café during the war affected women's social lives negatively. Yet Ilham herself, one of the regular customers of the prewar Express Café, did not go frequently to the new postwar cafés. She continued to look for the "right" café, though in the meantime, she said, "Every now and then I go to the City Café to meet friends or just to regain my ability to read the newspaper cover to cover." But the new cafés are different from those that existed in the past, she says; the atmosphere is not so welcoming and the prices are so expensive that intellectuals and middle-class customers could not afford it.

Another woman explained the phenomena of the increasing number of expensive restaurants and the decrease in the number of cafés as "a signifier of the decrease in the size of the middle class." She viewed this process as a deterioration in the position of women, since "women could go to the cafés alone, but they needed to be accompanied by a husband or a family member if they wanted to go to a restaurant." Many women who belonged to the middle class agreed that the prewar era was better for them.

REMEMBRANCES AND AMNESIA

As illustrated in the case of prewar cafés, the memories of these places became a shared, collective experience, especially for the educated middle-class intellectuals who had not been able to accept or adjust to the postwar spaces and social structures. They resorted to collective remembering to defy their marginalization and exclusion from the new plans and urban spaces.

Collective memory has become a common theme in the fields of anthropology, history, and cultural studies. Writings on the politics of remembering and forgetting were heavily influenced by the work of the French sociologist Maurice Halbwachs (1992) and theorist Pierre Nora (1989). Maurice Halbwachs first introduced the term "collective memory" in 1925 and defined it as "the way members of the community collectively imagine and recall their past" (1992, 38). Therefore, the social context of the present provided individuals with the raw materials for remembering and forgetting: "It is in society that people normally acquire their memories. It is also in society that they recall, recognize, and localize their memories" (Halbwachs 1992, 38).

Social scientists, both those who accepted and those who rejected Halbwachs' definition of collective memory, agree that individuals and groups recall selected moments of the past and suppress, forget, and silence other moments to cope with their present needs and future desires. Similarly, anthropologists make use of the concept of collective memory in societies that experienced colonialism, civil wars, and reconciliation processes. Richard Werbner, in his study *Memory and the Postcolony*, rejects Halbwachs' "presentist line" that reduced memory to "an artifact of the here and now, as if it were merely a backward construction after the fact." Instead, Werbner suggests that memory is complex because "the very passion in, for, and against memory, keeping it alive, burying or killing it, disclosing, registering, textualizing, and re-creating it, is also problematic in our analysis" (1998, 2–3). Similar to Werbner, in her study of East Madagascar, anthropologist Jennifer Cole also criticized earlier writings about the functions of collective remembering and argued that memory, including colonially shaped recollected past, is not merely a matter of negotiating power in the present but rather is a political tool and a vehicle of empowerment (1998). Women's memories were not addressed until the publication of a pivotal issue of *Signs*[7] in 2002 that looked at memory in gendered terms.

WARTIME SOCIAL SITES

As the war continued, most of Beirut's cafés were replaced with temporary coffee-drinking sites, funeral homes, and expresso vans. These mobile venues continued to exist for the entire period of the war, and some would continue even after it ended. They satisfied a specific social and political need and transformed the meaning of urban space.

The war altered the use and meaning of urban space in that places that were once familiar and accessible became prohibited and forbidden. The once-cosmopolitan Beirut became a symbol of war-torn divided cities. A clear demarcation, the "Green Line," a no-man's-land, divided Beirut into East-West and Christian-Muslim. With a few exceptions, many of those who lived on one side of the city never crossed this dividing line. As stated earlier, during the war years, East Beirut became foreign, unfamiliar, and inaccessible to most of those who lived in West Beirut, and vice versa. Therefore, the part of the city where residents were not allowed to enter or have homes was neither public nor private; rather, it was a "prohibited space."

Although the city was divided, some residents challenged the new order and found ways to cross from one side to the other. Sireena, a middle-class Christian woman who decided to stay in the predominately Muslim part, remembered her experiences when she used to cross the Green Line:

> Although I am Christian, I stayed in West Beirut where my house and work were located. After many of my friends and relatives had moved to the other side [the eastern, Christian part], I wanted to keep my relationship with them alive. I did not want to allow anybody to prevent me from moving around my own city. I had driven my car across the Green Line several times. Whenever I was asked to stop by a militia fighter, I would look him in the eye and say: "Look at my white hair; I am older than your mother!"

Passing the numerous militia-controlled checkpoints made crossing from one side of the city to the other a journey of suffering and danger. In an ironic reversal, it was now women who could move about the city with greater safety and ease than men. The militia tacitly agreed to ignore the movement of women. In effect, women became invisible to the militiamen, since they were not viewed as combatants or a potential danger.[8] Thus, women became the protectors of men when they escorted them across militia-controlled borders. In my field interviews, the women recalled this phase as empowering, even though their invisibility reminded them yet again of their absence from the political arena. Tellingly, men never mentioned these experiences in their own narrations of the war.[9] When women told me stories about their ability to move freely, men reacted with unease, laughing, interrupting the women, and dismissing their accounts or even accusing them of exaggerating their roles.

During the war, access to both "public" and "private" space was not necessarily predetermined by social and economic status; on the contrary, the affordability of space was based on personal connection to the militia in control of specific areas.[10] One woman who belonged to the upper middle class described her wartime neighbors:

> You knew they came from rural areas where they raised goats and chickens. They were not accustomed to living in city apartments. They had too many children, who fought and screamed day and night. Their noise annoyed me more than the noise of bombs. They even threw their garbage from the windows. I am so glad they are gone . . .

Upper- and middle-class Beirutis agonizingly described the deterioration in their standard of living as they were forced to share the city with members of the lower class who lacked urban culture.

THE TRADITIONAL COFFEEHOUSE (*AL-MAQHA*)

The traditional coffeehouse (*al-maqha*) is a prewar public space that is often recalled with nostalgia. Unlike the Western-style café that was open for both men and women who belonged to the middle class, an *al-maqha* functioned as a social club for men across class lines. In his memoir, Itani, an old Sunni Beiruti lawyer, suggested that the traditional coffeehouses were categorized according to their location within the city. The location determined the kind of customers who frequented the coffeehouses as well as the activities that took place in them. He listed three kinds of traditional coffeehouses in Beirut: (1) the beach coffeehouses, like al-Ḥaj Dawood and al-Ghalayini, that functioned as meeting sites for sailors, merchants, and tourists; (2) coffeehouses like al-Qazaz, Falasteen, and al-Farouq that were located at the heart of the city center and frequented mostly by the workers in the area and men who came to Beirut from the countryside; (3) the port coffeehouses that catered to fishermen, port workers, and sailors.[11]

The traditional coffeehouse (*al-maqha*) served water-pipe (*argileh*); Turkish coffee; tea; "traditional" cold drinks such as lemonade, *jellab* (a drink made of dates and nuts), and licorice juice; and appetizers. Interestingly, in his description of the coffee-drinking scene in Beirut, Itani overlooked one type, the modern French cafés located in the Ras Beirut area. However, when I talked to intellectuals—men and women, Lebanese and non-Lebanese—about their prewar café experiences, most of them mentioned only the modern cafés of Hamra Street.

FUNERAL HOMES (*BAYT AL-AJER*)

During the war, Beirutis had expected to be killed at any moment by snipers, rockets, or car bombs. The fear of sudden death created a temporary sense of community among those who stayed in the city. This shared experience of facing an unpredictable danger turned funeral homes into sites of activities and social gatherings.

Before the war, funerals were usually held for three days at the home of the deceased person; but during the war, private houses were not large enough to accommodate all those who came to pay condolences. As an alternative, a number of specialized funeral homes were created out of diverse urban spaces: the Shiʿite mosque known as the *ḥusayniyah*,[12] building basements, abandoned buildings, parking lots, or the street itself were all used as temporary funeral homes for the mourning families.

Then women from across generations, religious affiliations, and educational and social classes all found emotional solace in attending funerals for three days.

One of the women I interviewed said:

> I had never been to a funeral [before the war] . . . but [during the war] I found myself traveling from one funeral home to the other. . . . It became a war habit. I went to some funerals of people that I knew and to many for those whom I did not even know. Sometimes, I would leave the funeral and then ask about the name of the deceased person!

Another woman said:

> I used to go to funerals to assure myself that I was still alive! And that it was someone else who got killed . . .

A third said:

> It was a chance to wail for my own miseries while everybody was crying about theirs . . . (*kulun yabiku ʿala mawtahum*).

Although funeral sites were segregated based on gender, they were integrated across social classes. Funerals became the wartime coffee-drinking spaces for women that then lingered on into the postwar period.

Amal explained the advantages of going to funerals during the war by saying:

> During funeral days, . . . you were always welcomed. No one could ask you to leave; no appointment was necessary; you had the chance to

meet many people, hear the latest news and gossip about who died, who left the country, who moved somewhere else, and who stayed behind.

In 1997, six years after the end of the war, I attended a funeral. Abu Adel, a man from humble origins, had died the day before, after suffering from a long illness. In two large rooms that opened onto each other, the widow, Um Adel; her three daughters; and her daughter-in-law sat in their chairs facing the entrance to the apartment. For the occasion, the five women had covered their heads with thin black scarves. As Um Adel's grandchildren ate potato chips and played around the room, other women occupied the chairs surrounding the grieving family. There were a number of empty chairs around the perimeter of the large room, and a male voice reciting the Quran from a tape recorder filled the room.

Women, who arrived in groups of two or three, expressed sympathy to the grieving relatives, hugged and kissed them. Although the sons of the deceased were not present at the women's section of the funeral home, most of the women repeated the same phrases: "Those who reproduced [sons] did not die (*yali khalaf ma mat*); or "May God grant long lives to his sons (*toul al-'ummur li-wladu*). Then, the women somberly walked around the room, shook the hands of the rest of the visitors, and took the empty seats. Three teenage girls, relatives of Um Adel, served bitter traditional Arabic coffee to the guests. In the middle of the room, a number of small tables were arranged on which lay a selection of cigarette boxes. The women drank their coffee, smoked cigarettes, and talked to whoever was sitting next to them. Every now and then, some entered into conversation with other women sitting far across the room, and asked loudly for news of people that they knew in common.

Following Islamic traditions, Abu Adel was buried on the same day he died, and his family rented a nearby empty apartment to receive guests for three days. Later, the widow told me that she had debated with her sons and daughters whether to rent a place or to receive the guests at their home. Um Adel said that since the war, many families stopped renting places for their funerals because now fewer people tend to attend them. She then explained the reasons that made her rent a place instead of holding the funeral at home:

> We were not sure how many people would come. We knew that nowadays it is different from wartime, but we were not sure how different. In the end, we decided to rent a place. I am pleased we did so. Hundreds of relatives and friends showed up, some of whom we had not seen for years. During the war, my husband and I went to the funerals of both

relatives and strangers (*al-qurub wa al-ghurob*). Now these people are paying us back our visits.

For the family of the deceased, receiving hundreds of guests was a social obligation and a form of reciprocity. Women's reasons for attending funerals both during the war and in its aftermath were different from those of men. Funeral homes provided a "public" space for women to visit and socialize that was free from the obligation of the direct gift exchange expected on other occasions.

Although wartime funeral homes and prewar cafés shared spatial similarities, the gender, class, and sectarian identities of those who attended them were different. In the funeral home, women were segregated from men, but they were more integrated across class and religion. In contrast to funeral home experiences, women who possessed the cultural and economic capital were able to frequent Hamra Street cafés regardless of their sectarian affiliation.

Women's spatial experiences at the cafés and funeral homes refute the simple dichotomies of private-public and feminine-masculine. The funeral home was a temporary place that opened only three days for each deceased person. This means that Amal's choice to go and pay condolences and socialize with others was determined by the occurrence of a death. Thus the funeral site became a temporary mobile social space in contrast to the greater stability and permanence of the café. Unlike the café, the funeral home was an accessible public space for women from different economic and social backgrounds, whereas the café scene was mapped according to the political, social, and economic affiliation of its respective clients.

EXPRESSO VANS: TEMPORARY SOCIALIZING

Unlike women, men who attended funerals found additional temporary civilian sites for gathering, socializing, and coffee drinking. Mobile expresso vans became some of the most popular social venues for men. Two years into the war, after almost all the cafés closed, the phenomenon of the expresso van started, and it lasted for the whole period of the war. Some of them still continued to sell coffee a few years after the war ended. The van owners, the majority of whom were from rural areas, chose this as a "safe" form of work, because it kept them close to their families and away from direct fighting and provided a regular source of income.

Although these vans were frequented by many Beirutis, residents of wealthy neighborhoods regarded them as signs of deterioration and as a reminder of the war. The heroine in Layla Ussayran's novel *A Bird from the Moon: A Story about Beirut* mournfully reports the sudden emergence of these coffee vehicles:

> A new neighborhood emerged—on the seashore [the Corniche] but this time, it was made of lines of small vans that carried espresso coffee machines. People continued their habit of drinking coffee, but this time they were drinking it from plastic cups, sitting on folding chairs . . .

The plastic cup innovation was contrasted with the old days "when the coffee man clinked his ceramic cups with one hand, and carried his authentic brass coffeepot on his other shoulder" (Ussayran 1996, 45–46).

With fewer cafés during the war, men—Christian, Muslim, militia or nonmilitia, rich and poor—all started to gather around the mobile expresso vans on folding chairs, and the vans moved from location to location on a regular basis. Omar, who owned a small stationary store near Corniche Street, told me:

> I used to spend many hours sitting around "el-Exbress." During the war, we had plenty of time to waste. There I saw my friends, played cards, discussed politics, and watched football games. There were vans of all colors, models, and sizes lined up next to each other on Corniche, and we chose the one that we liked the most.

Since the price of coffee was affordable, the vans created a male egalitarian space that Omar characterized as a place "where no one could brag about his wealth." Or as a friend of Omar explained: "If someone was accompanied by one hundred Sri Lankan maids[13] or one hundred dogs, no one would have paid attention to him, because the seashore had been there for all people and everyone could afford to pay for his coffee." Omar saw the coffee van as a site of social equality.

Abu Talal, a Shiʿite from a village in South Lebanon, operated one of the most popular vans in the area for fifteen years. Before running the coffee van, Abu Talal had worked in various venues: a jewelry shop, a blacksmith workshop, and as a truck driver. Abu Talal proudly declared that he had never made a cup of coffee when he first bought the van, so initially he was forced to hire someone to help him prepare the coffee. Yet he insisted on following what he considered the highest standards in making coffee. Using the word "Nescafé" to mean instant coffee, he then said: "I bought the best coffee in the market; for the 'Nescafé,' I only used Maxwell House, and Nestlé instant milk. I did not go for the cheap stuff."

As a van operator, Abu Talal created a social atmosphere for himself and for his customers. He controlled the sidewalk around his van, which Omar and his friends described as a public space. Abu Talal thus privatized parts of one of the most public spaces of the city: the street. The area surrounding the van "belonged" to Abu Talal, which meant that he was responsible for keeping it clean and protecting its reputation. He proudly mentioned that he had fired a worker for dealing hashish. When I asked Abu Talal, "Did women frequent the coffee vans?" he answered:

> Occasionally, my wife and daughters used to come and sit around the van. This encouraged other women in the area to feel comfortable to come and have their coffee there. I treated them as my sisters, and my customers did the same. I never allowed ill-mannered behaviors around my van.

Perhaps this was true of Abu Talal's van, but when I asked various women about these venues, they did not necessarily remember them as spaces for socializing. Some said they would stop by to buy a coffee and then walk away, but none of them told stories about socializing around the vans.

By the end of the war, there were over 110 coffee vans on Corniche Street. These vans competed with each other in many ways, and in fact some of them dispensed items other than coffee. Those who frequented the vans recalled incidents where the van owners had sold fish they caught from the sea or illegal drugs, and some even operated prostitution rings.

In the aftermath of the war, the government attempted to create an orderly city and erase the irregularities of wartime. The municipality tried to regulate the coffee vans a number of times. The first action was to make all the operators paint their vans white. Next, they were required to get a license plate with an official city number, necessitating fees and taxes, then a corner was assigned for each van, and a fixed distance of seventy-five meters was established between the parked vans.

These efforts to legalize the war's irregularities could be read as an attempt to put an end to the war. Ironically, the municipality's regulations were also temporary. In 1997, and after this licensing decree, the municipality decided to eject all the expresso vans. These actions provoked the owners to organize and to negotiate for more rights. More than eighty van owners brought their children and wives to a demonstration at the house of Prime Minister Hariri. According to one of the organizers:

We made the women and children walk at the front of the demonstration so the police and the army wouldn't do harm. Also, we wanted to convey the message to the prime minister that removing the vans would starve our families.

The strategy failed: Police beat the women and children. Unlike during the war, women were unable to protect the men at these moments of danger.

After lengthy negotiations with the van owners, the municipality allowed the licensed vans to operate but not on the Corniche. Additionally, the vans were not allowed to use chairs or to utilize the public street for their private business. They were ordered to find private property and work from there, a decree that presented a considerable challenge for the van owners. Their response was to find yet another temporary strategy: they parked in front of destroyed or abandoned buildings. The official policies thus successfully redefined private and public spaces, with dramatic consequences for daily social practices.

CONCLUDING REMARKS

Beiruti women and men remembered prewar and wartime coffee-drinking venues to counter the collective amnesia imposed on them by the government and the private sector. While middle-class educated women passionately recollected their social interactions at Western-style cafés located in the Hamra District—then a modern neighborhood located outside the crowded downtown area—working-class men recalled their days in the traditional coffeehouses located in the commercial districts. When these coffee-drinking public sites became off-limits during the war, Beirutis drank their coffee and socialized in the temporary wartime ad hoc semipublic sites of the funeral homes and the mobile expresso vans. Unlike the prewar time, when middle-class men and women socialized in the same Western cafés, during the war the groups were demarcated across gender lines.

Unlike 'Ayn el-Mreisse tenants and the neighborhood collectives who fought the postwar unpredictability of private space through political means, the people discussed in this chapter responded to their loss of public sites in a passive way and individually. Some of the same people, in fact, did struggle actively and collectively over their apartments, but the same kind of strategic intervention never emerged around purely social spaces like cafés. Instead, the now-nonexistent prewar and wartime coffee-drinking sites became sites of longing, and even escapes from the alienation of the present.

The next chapter leaves coffee venues to return to dwellings, but for a much more marginal group than the tenants and coffee drinkers discussed above: the war-displaced. Though disenfranchised, the displaced found active strategies for dealing with postwar uncertainty, defying their marginalization by employing legal and illegal means to secure urban spaces lost to development.

In an attempt to establish legitimacy after the chaos of the long war in Beirut, the Hariri government tried to restore state institutions and re-claim its role as a legitimate authority. The new government, in addition to the functions of its day-to-day operations, had to resolve a host of byproducts of the war, including giving financial aid to the thousands of displaced families. This task was part of an effort to incorporate the war militias into postwar communities, to reconcile opposing sectarian and political groups, and to forge one unified history among the multiple ethnoreligious groups. The government now gave priority to the rebuild-ing of Beirut's Central District, and to accomplish this, the city had to remove the displaced who lived there.

A song by the renowned Lebanese singer Ziad al-Rahbani touches the issue of the displaced:

Kan fi 'indna bayt shi'er ejo al-mhajareen a'adoo fi. (Once we had a line [lit-erally, "house"] of poetry; the displaced came and occupied it.)

Al-Rahbani's lyric plays on a literary pun, in that parts of poetry are called by names for parts of residences: what English calls a "line" of poetry is called in Arabic a "house" of poetry. Hence the connotation of al-Rahbani's line is that those displaced by the war are taking over all kinds of spaces in the city, even symbolic, literary, or cultural spaces. His poetic expression aptly summarizes a prevalent attitude in postwar Beirut. I heard variations of that phrase for the first time from property owners in the city, who quoted the lyric to complain about their own present situa-tion. The landlords then maneuvered to evict the displaced, who had fled their original homes, primarily in the rural south, and become squatters in private apartments and other spaces.

This chapter gives an ethnographic account of those displaced by the war, people who occupied a "liminal" position in the postwar era. This account reconstructs the attitudes of the nondisplaced and the experiences of the displaced themselves. It emphasizes three main points. First, the physical rebuilding of downtown Beirut marginalized the displaced by excluding them from the plans for the future city, in effect displacing them yet one more time in the postwar era. Second, these processes of inclusion and exclusion shaped the ways in which the displaced shaped their own narratives of the past. Third, these narratives, in turn, affected the social, political, and symbolic meanings of the spaces they used.

Space in postwar Beirut was and remains sharply contested, and that dispute engendered profound changes in social definitions of urban space. The conflicts over space touched every level of society: family members, neighbors, religious or political groups, militia members, the postwar government, and the investors and developers. Competitors struggled not only over who had access to space and how it was to be used but over how these places were to be preserved and represented. This competition brought about significant shifts in conceptions of collective identity, especially regarding the construction of alternative collectivities and alliances. In other words, new maps of inclusion and exclusion, or self and other in everyday life, came into being in postwar Beirut.

The plight of the displaced illustrated that power relationships were both embedded in and manifested through the struggle over urban sites and spaces, even though the war had ended in 1991. In the late 1990s, the displaced were still a marginalized population who lived in a transitional situation. However, to cope with or even to overcome their liminality, the displaced developed strategies to involve themselves in the debates surrounding Beirut's reconstruction project. Because their primary interest was to secure permanent homes, they also relied on their prewar and war experiences to claim rootedness in the city.

I describe how this marginal population, the displaced, developed strategies to negotiate for spatial rights from landlords and government agencies, how they deployed and manipulated their own accounts of prewar and wartime experiences to evade eviction or gain cash compensation, and how they used political and social networks to demonstrate their rights to specific places.

PREWAR MIGRATION AND WARTIME DISPLACEMENT

Prior to the war in 1975, thousands of peasants seeking job opportunities had migrated from their ancestral villages to Beirut.[1] The majority of these migrants exchanged farming for unskilled low-paying urban jobs in the capital. Upon their arrival in Beirut, immigrant families joined other relatives in overcrowded poor neighborhoods. Later, during the war, more displacement occurred, and many of these same immigrants were forced to leave their homes one more time.

During the war, both Muslims and Christians were forced to flee their original neighborhoods and join their respective sectarian groups in other parts of the city, because Beirut was divided in two, Christians in the east and Muslims in the west. Thus, thousands of residents joined their presumed religious groups during this time. Additionally, waves of displaced peasants from South Lebanon and the Chūf Mountains sought refuge in Beirut at different times during the war. Although a few thousand of the displaced from South Lebanon had arrived in Beirut prior to 1975, their number swelled during the war and even continued in its aftermath. As a result of the recurrent Israeli attacks on South Lebanon in 1969, 1975, 1993, 1996, and 2006,[2] waves of displaced villagers continued to arrive in the city. Furthermore, the Israeli occupation of South Lebanon from 1978 until 2000 prevented the displaced from returning to their villages. It is estimated that half of the Lebanese population was temporarily or permanently forced to evacuate their homes during the sixteen years of war (Charif 1994; Faour 1991; Peleikis 2001).

Unlike the poor peasants, a large number of the country's elite sought voluntary exile in neighboring Arab countries, France, the United States, Canada, Australia, and even West African countries, and thus joined the already existing Lebanese diaspora. After the war, some of those exiled Lebanese returned to reclaim apartments and houses they had left locked but which in the intervening years had been occupied by the internally displaced. The interests of the returning elite matched the interests of both Solidere and the government plans to cleanse the city of the "illegal" war squatters.

However, the process of evacuating the displaced did not begin only after the war. In fact, negotiations between the squatters and property owners had already taken place both during and immediately after the war. Some landlords managed on their own to evict the occupants who paid nothing or very low rent. These owners employed various means to repossess their properties; one method was to physically evict the squatters without compensation by enlisting the power of militias or the Syrian army. The second, less favorable strategy was to negotiate cash compensations. Either way, the actions of these landlords placed the displaced population in precarious conditions.

Rooftop view of apartment buildings in Beirut

UM NIZAR AND MULTIPLE DISPLACEMENTS

The story of Um Nizar and her family illustrates the ongoing struggles of the displaced. Before the civil war (1975–1991), Um Nizar, her husband, and their four children lived in their ancestral Druze village in the mountains overlooking Beirut. The family moved to Beirut in 1970, seeking economic opportunities and an education for their children. There, they lived with relatives for five years in East Beirut. In 1975, the outbreak of the war forced Um Nizar's family to return to their village in the Chūf Mountains. However, two years later, they were forced to leave the village again after the Maronite Christian and Druze militiamen began to fight each other. They returned to Beirut, but this time to ʿAyn el-Mreisse, a predominantly Muslim neighborhood. Now, Um Nizar was forced to share residence with other families, sometimes even in nonresidential spaces.

Initially, Um Nizar shared a two-bedroom apartment with members of her extended family. Only later, when her relatives were entrusted by a Christian family with keys for another apartment, did Um Nizar have her own apartment. Um Nizar's husband, Abu Nizar, had worked as a taxi driver and grocer, but because of the war, he felt compelled to join a neighborhood militia. He was eventually killed in battle. Um Nizar, now a widow and the sole breadwinner, had to scramble for housing after the building she lived in was hit by a rocket during the 1982 Israeli invasion. This time, with the help of a charitable organization, she was able to settle into a hotel room in the destroyed city center and had to share a bathroom and cooking facilities with several other families. Later, after securing employment at a hospital, she managed to move back to an apartment in 'Ayn el-Mreisse with the help of her husband's militia. As we can see, Um Nizar's experience was one of repeated dislocation and an ongoing struggle for stability in the face of violence. This journey to find a suitable home was typical of many of the displaced during the war. They often bounced from one place to another without staying long enough to settle down. This uprooted population operated through informal networks in this ad hoc war economy and had to rely on the assistance of charitable organizations, militias, or relatives.

Um Nizar's seemingly never-ending quest for shelter continued even after the war. The insecurity and violence experienced by families such as hers did not abate even when the war ended in 1991, despite the expressed determination of the postwar government to create unity and "heal the wounds of the war." Quite the reverse, the reconstruction of downtown Beirut resulted in more displacement. Whereas during the war these families had often been able to access resources using legal, illegal, formal, and informal means, the postwar conditions increasingly forced them into social and economic marginality.

AGENCIES AND INTEREST GROUPS
DEALING WITH THE DISPLACED

The predicament of families such as Um Nizar's became a priority for the postwar government. To adjust the status of thousands of these cases and to coordinate the work of the multiple players dealing with issues of displacement, the government established two temporary governmental agencies: the Ministry of the Displaced and the Central Fund for the Displaced. These agencies were mandated to negotiate between the two disputing camps: the displaced and their political representatives[3] on the one hand, and property owners, investors, and developers such as Solidere on the other. The majority of the latter group agreed that displaced families needed to be cleared from the spaces they were occupying, believing that eliminating their presence would help "heal the wounds of the war."

However, the different authorities could not agree on a method that would resolve the problem. During the war and immediately after the ceasefire, before the state had solidified, it became customary for property owners to pay the displaced an evacuation fee known as *khliw*. In the early 1990s, Solidere also adopted this arrangement of reimbursing the displaced so as to swiftly initiate the reconstruction of the downtown area. Solidere's ad hoc strategy prompted the newly formed government agencies to create a more comprehensive policy toward the displaced. After much deliberation, Solidere, the representatives of the displaced,[4] and governmental agencies were able to reach a consensus. They decided that "all 'qualified' displaced were to be paid cash compensation for evacuating the public and private properties they had been occupying since the war."[5] The funds were pooled from both governmental and private sources and were to be dispensed through the Central Fund of the Displaced and the Ministry of the Displaced.

The Ministry of the Displaced had three main responsibilities: supervising the return of thousands of the displaced to their prewar homes, responding to their emerging daily concerns and needs, and negotiating appropriate compensation for their cooperation in vacating occupied properties. Later on, and under increasing pressure from Solidere, the Central Fund for the Displaced was also established to further expedite this transition of the displaced from the greater Beirut area. This fund handled the claims on behalf of the Ministry of the Displaced, Solidere, and property owners.

DEFINING AND COUNTING THE DISPLACED

Among the challenges faced by the institutions coordinating the efforts to evacuate the displaced was the need to define who was a displaced person in order to determine the size of this population and then allocate the needed funds. The word "displaced" (*muhajjareen*) derives from the root verb *hajara*, which literally means "to migrate" or "to leave by force." The word *hajara*, an equivalent to the English passive (past participle), suggests that the act of displacement itself was imposed. Furthermore, the use of the passive voice implies that the displaced were not agents of their own situation, but rather were victims of the war. Governmental agencies, journalists, and the displaced themselves as well as their representatives used the word *muhajjareen* to garner public sympathy. However, to the native Beirutis, the same term, "displaced" (*muhajjareen*), had a derogatory connotation, despite its inherent suggestion of victimhood.

Another term, "occupiers" (*muhtaleen*), was used widely by owners of the illegally occupied properties and prewar residents of the city to describe the displaced. (The similar beginning of both words, *mu*, is not indicative of shared meaning, but only of its grammatical structure as a nominalizing prefix.) The use of the word "occupier" instead of "displaced" reconceptualized those in question not as passive victims, but as illegal usurpers, outsiders, and actors with full agency, therefore casting them as the cause of the problem. In fact, the term rendered property owners themselves as victims of the "occupiers."

After much debate, the Ministry of the Displaced defined the displaced person (*al-muhajjar*) as "any individual, Lebanese or non-Lebanese national, who lives on Lebanese soil and has been affected by the war and hindered by its consequences from enjoying his or her full legal and civil rights to the house and properties from which he or she was displaced" (The Lebanese Ministry of the Displaced 1996, 5).

According to the ministry's definition, most of those who lived in Lebanon during the war would have fallen into this category,[6] since many could present persuasive evidence that they had been uprooted at least once as a result of the conflict. Despite the imprecision of its formal definition, the ministry operated according to a more specific definition, which was revealed to me in the course of my research. In my field interviews, I was informed by officials at the Ministry of the Displaced that in fact the displaced were only those who after the war continued to occupy spaces they did not legally own or lease. But the ambiguity of the printed definition led to many abuses. Many agencies and the displaced themselves were able to submit applications for compensation even for individuals who by then had regular housing.

There was no solid agreement on fundamental facts, such as how many displaced there were or what constituted displacement. The Ministry of the Displaced calculated the toll of the war in the following report:

> 90,000 families[7] had been displaced, with an average of 5.7 persons in each family. 180,000 homes were completely destroyed, and many were seriously damaged. 45,000 families illegally occupied the homes of other families. 12,000 families lived in dwellings not designated for human habitation, such as commercial buildings, industrial centers, and buildings liable to collapse. (The Lebanese Ministry of the Displaced 1996, 9)

However, there was not complete agreement on the exact figures; some adopted the ministry's definition and estimates, while many others drafted their own estimates and definitions. Lebanese researchers working on the issue, for example, contested the ministry's figures. When I interviewed Khalil Abu Rjeileh,[8] a social scientist at the Lebanese University who also identified himself as a displaced person, he estimated the number of the displaced at around 860,000, over 100,000 more than the ministry's figure of 750,000. Abu Rjeileh accounted for the discrepancy in two ways. First, the ministry gave the displaced only two months in which to file claims; hence, many families, especially those living outside the country, did not have enough time to meet the proposed deadline. The second involved sectarian politics. Many Christians, who did not recognize the postwar government, were instructed by the leaders of their sectarian groups not to participate in filing for compensation; thus a sizable population of displaced Christians was excluded from the ministry's estimate but included within Abu Rjeileh's number.

In addition to contesting the number of displaced and the very definition of displacement, one heard various delineations drawn between the legitimate and illegitimate, or real and fake, displaced. Abu Rjeileh distinguishes between the real displaced (*muhajjareen*) and the occupiers (*muhtaleen*). For him, many of those who filed claims for compensation were in fact occupiers because they owned homes somewhere else while they illegally occupied other people's properties. When I asked him why people would occupy a house when they already owned one, Abu Rjeileh argued that because the "occupiers" lacked morals, they abused the compensation system. He explained:

> The real displaced persons fled to Beirut from rural areas during the war. At that time, the majority of them stayed in schools and public buildings. Most of them evacuated these places soon after the war because they had self-respect and respected private property. Thus, they did not take over the property of others. But the "occupiers" who filed claims as displaced persons were in fact wartime militia members, who themselves forced people out of their homes during the war.[9]

According to this analysis, the "actual" displaced were victims of the war who respected private property. In this moral scheme, these real displaced had a legal right to use certain spaces, "empty" public buildings, but not privately owned commercial or residential ones. Abu Rjeileh questioned the ethics and morality of some of the displaced who filed for compensation. He believed the occupiers were nothing more than members of the militia who destroyed the country and later abused its resources after the war.

The dominant attitude toward the displaced was manifested in the public discourse that defined them. Property owners and city residents often viewed the displaced as an obstacle to the rejuvenation of the city. They were depicted as uncivilized peasants who lacked urban character, and their continued presence would harm the so-called "cosmopolitan" and "civilized" Beirut. Governmental agencies shared a similar vision that the presence of this population was a major obstacle to "healing the wounds of war." Many officials argued that in order to return to the prewar state of normalcy, the city must be "cleansed" of all vestiges of the war, and therefore the displaced were mandated to leave the city. Generally speaking, all the proposed solutions included giving cash compensation to the displaced for vacating occupied properties. Agencies and groups who worked closely with this population expected them to return to their former homes, which were mostly located outside the city. Thus, despite the strong desire of the displaced to remain in the city, the government did not provide alternative housing either in Beirut or even outside it. However, after receiving the compensation, instead of returning to their prewar homes, many of the displaced moved to the Southern Suburb of Beirut, which devolved into squatter areas and became a new urban problem.

The debate over "cleansing" the city was often accompanied by discourses of modernity, urban planning, rebuilding, and reconstruction. The presence of these refugees was seen as a serious obstacle to the implementation of reconstruction agendas and modernity itself. The displaced were even accused of disturbing the social order and making the city dirty and uncivilized. The process of modernization included cleaning and organizing disordered spaces, vacating illegally occupied buildings, and granting more power to the private sector. However, this attempt at aesthetic renewal resulted in new unequal power relations.

Officials appointed to solve the plight of the displaced often shared a negative view of this population. This vision resulted in the mismanagement of the allocated funds, and this intensified the state of liminality of the displaced. When I interviewed Kareem, a high official at the Central Fund for the Displaced, he summarized the administration's position: "When we started the evacuation process, we found families living in uninhabitable conditions. The walls were torn out, the windows were boarded up or covered with plastic sheets, and there was no running water. Do you want me to believe their claims of residency?" Kareem strongly believed that these families had illegally moved into these spaces after they had learned that compensation was possible. He then described the rampant abuse of this process by the displaced at one building, which housed the Rivoli Theater, located next to Martyrs' Square. This building was a grand two-story structure with high ceilings and a large hall surrounded by 150 offices and forty shops. Kareem described the magnitude of the abuse:

> The building cannot accommodate more than two hundred families by any means. [Yet] for this location alone we received claims from more than one thousand families. When people heard about the compensation, the buses started unloading men, women, and children of all ages at the Rivoli Theater building. They were mostly relatives who came from the same village. Initially, there were a few daily workers [single men] who lived there temporarily, and then they invited their families and relatives after they learned of the compensation.

Kareem described many of the families that were awarded compensation as "fictitious." He pointed to the so-called "hard evidence" of physical dimensions, religious beliefs, and ethical concerns to substantiate his deductions:

> I myself accompanied the team to evict the displaced from a rundown studio apartment in the downtown area. Although the walls were covered with posters of naked women, nine religious Muslim families had claimed residency in a thirty-square-meter room. Now, tell me, how did they manage to sleep there? Why would conservative Shi'ite families hang posters of naked women? . . . Despite all of this, we issued them their checks.

Here, Kareem viewed the displaced as uncivilized citizens lacking moral values. Although his agency, the Central Fund for the Displaced, issued the compensation, he was sure that their claims were false, and his proof was the exaggerated number of families who shared a room decorated with posters of naked women.

Basim, another government official who worked with this population, shared a similarly cynical opinion. He even attributed what he called the "new displacement" to the compensation process. He revealed that they had evicted families who came from villages that did not experience actual fighting or forced migration. Using a sarcastic tone and moving his hand in a dismissive gesture, he added: "They squatted in Beirut because they thought they would make money or perhaps for the sake of breathing fresh air (*sham hawa*).[10] I am pretty sure that they became displaced two days before they applied for compensation. We received thousands of applications, two or three times more than we had anticipated." Government officials found themselves obliged to participate in these fraudulent schemes because of the coercion of high-ranking politicians.

Government officials also viewed the displaced as irresponsible peasants who were unable to make wise decisions as to how the money should be spent. Additionally, they were viewed as disloyal citizens whose ill-advised spending practices did not contribute to the economy of their country. Thus, the displaced were seen as ignorant of what was in their best interest and that of their country. One financial consultant I interviewed said that the money that was paid to the displaced was a total waste. According to him:

> The displaced are limited culturally and educationally. However, they managed to obtain a good amount of money, both legally and illegally. Do you know what they did with the compensation? The money was spent on "dead" useless objects. They married a second wife, bought her gold, and bought themselves expensive cars and mobile phones. Of course, they did not even entertain the idea of buying houses or starting businesses. If they had been wise, they would not be sitting here unemployed and the money would have revived the economy. Marrying a second wife and buying gold is a total waste.

In the past few years, anthropologists have begun to theorize about nationalism and displacements. Authors argued that because the displaced are often viewed as a population without a legitimate space, they live in liminality, a state of "betwixt and between" (Turner 1967, 97). In *Purity and Exile*, Liisa Malkki discusses the systematic invisibility of refugees in the buildup of nations:

> They are not seen as representatives of any particular local culture and they have lost a kind of imagined cultural authority to stand for "their kind" or for the imagined whole of which they are or were part. (1997, 7)

Malkki explained the exclusion of refugees in anthropological analysis by citing Turner's idea that refugees are considered "transitional beings and are particularly polluting, since they are neither one thing nor another; or may be both; or neither here nor there; or may even be nowhere in terms of any recognized cultural topography. Refugees are seen to hemorrhage or weaken national boundaries and to pose a threat to the 'national security'" (1997, 7). In Lebanon, the displaced were viewed as a constant reminder of the war and as an obstacle to the return to prewar glory. Governmental agencies, developers, and city residents all agreed that the displaced should be evicted from Beirut.

INTELLECTUALS CRITICIZE THE RETURN PLAN

Lebanese intellectuals and concerned individuals opposed the government's compensation policy and instead urged officials to resettle the refugee families in government-managed housing projects. Others suggested an alternative plan of providing construction materials that would allow the displaced to rebuild their homes in their ancestral villages. In this way, they criticized the government's policies, which gave priority to private investors and entrepreneurs while the interests of the general public were ignored and violated (Corm 1996; Salam 1998; Tabet 1996). These critics viewed cash compensation as a provisional solution designed to allow the private sector to carry out its investment projects without taking into consideration its long-term consequences. The sociologist Nabil Beyhum denounced these plans because they did not address the social problems related to postwar migration. According to him, "The project will not bring the end of displacement. On the contrary, it could provoke more displacement" (Beyhum, Salam, and Tabet 1994, 21–22). In his analysis of these policies, Beyhum expressed concern for future urban chaos caused by further relocation, which would in turn create new slums and unplanned neighborhoods.

However, other intellectual voices were less sympathetic toward the problem of displacement. In his study *The Suspended City*, Waddah Shararah described the displaced as temporary residents who imposed their "authentic rural culture" on the urban environment in which they now lived without necessarily integrating into its social life. He accused them of contaminating Beirut's urban heritage by "ruralizing" it and by literally violating it through violence (1985, 13–15). This opinion was only one segment of a wider public discourse. The Lebanese media and its daily newspapers addressed these issues on a daily basis and often presented the displaced as an obstacle to ending the war. The media also depicted the displaced as violent outsiders who did not belong to the city. Newspapers described the displaced as undisciplined intruders responsible for instability and chaos:

> The number of occupiers is doubling. There is chaos in registering the names [of the displaced]; 750 families became 2,500. (*Annahar*, June 25, 1996, 8)

> Three civilians and fourteen policemen were injured in the Kintari confrontations. The residents have asked to stop the explosives in the Venecia Tunnel. However, the Central Fund for the Displaced promised to solve the problem. (*Annahar*, January 28, 1997, 12)

These kinds of descriptions of the undeserving displaced were reproduced in the media and in ordinary conversation. Stories were published in newspapers recounting cases of displaced families who abused the compensation system and received large amounts of money based solely on nepotism and political connections. The neighborhood of Wadi Abu Jmīl, for example, was mockingly dubbed "the valley of gold" (Wadi al-Dahab), a nickname that suggested the questionable and excessive payments awarded to favorites of the political parties. I heard rumors that families in this area had received close to 100,000 dollars in compensation. This was also true in Ḥay Līf, another neighborhood, where it was reported that although sixty-five families had initially been identified as displaced, by the time of evacuation, three hundred families had been compensated.[11] After that, Ḥay Līf was dubbed "Bank Līf."

Daily newspapers reported a number of violent confrontations when the displaced refused to leave the properties they were occupying. In some of these cases, representatives of the Central Fund for the Displaced summoned the police to carry out the evictions. In 1996, local newspapers reported a case of "accidental violence" in which a building occupied by displaced families collapsed, killing a family of six. The family had continued to occupy the building while awaiting the promised compensation. The accident took place when Solidere dynamited an adjacent building. The suffering of the victims did not draw much sympathy. When I asked an official at the Central Fund for the Displaced about this incident, he blamed the surviving father for the death of his family. He commented: "While he [the father] was bargaining for higher compensation, the building had collapsed and killed his wife and children. He was not satisfied with the compensation he was offered; he wanted more!"

In the end, this confusion, the uncertainty, and the air of secrecy exacerbated the problems of the displaced and their relationship to the organizations handling their claims and those of the rest of the city residents.

THE DISPLACED MANIPULATING THE SYSTEM

The images of the displaced that circulated in the mainstream culture were entwined with the self-image and the practices of the displaced themselves. The accounts of these outrageous awards, despite their dubious authenticity and their negative connotation, had the unintended effect of raising the expectations of the displaced. Because of these rumors, many families who had already completed the process considered themselves unfairly paid. On the other hand, those who were still engaged in the process continued their search for connections to maximize their gain.

The lack of transparency in the evacuation process made the issue of displacement a highly politicized matter and one that everyone attempted to manipulate for their own benefit. Political parties conducted their own surveys to claim higher compensation for their members. The leader of 'Ayn el-Mreisse's chapter of the Amal Movement showed me long lists of names of displaced families, according to which some apartments were shared by six families and some single rooms by two families—numbers that seem impossible even in these strained postwar conditions. In 1996, in exchange for votes, candidates for parliament helped families file late applications for compensation and used their influence to have these accepted. Politicians on all sides accused one another of rechanneling money intended for the "real displaced" to their followers who were not legitimately displaced.

The displaced themselves also accused each other of abusing the compensation system. Displaced families in 'Ayn el-Mreisse, for example, accused those who lived in nearby Wadi Abu Jmīl of being able to obtain the highest amounts of money simply because their neighborhood was the last in the evacuation program. By the time the program reached Wadi Abu Jmīl, the political parties and displaced dwellers who had witnessed the process as it unfolded in other neighborhoods were better primed to protect their interests. The political parties advised their constituencies not to abandon the occupied properties without getting higher compensation.[12]

The following case of Um Hussein demonstrates the complexity and the secrecy involved in the eviction process. It points to the channels the displaced were forced to utilize to secure material gains. The representative of the Amal Movement in 'Ayn el-Mreisse had advised me to visit this family to see the harsh living conditions of the displaced while they awaited the promised compensation.

I arrived at Um Hussein's home in the morning of a humid summer day. The three-bedroom apartment was almost empty, except for some broken chairs, a couple of foam mattresses, and a few empty cardboard boxes scattered on the dirty floor. The glass windows had been replaced with thick blue plastic sheets, the poorly painted walls showed several cracks, and the kitchen was almost empty except for an old refrigerator and a stove burner with a few pots and dishes. Um Hussein, in her late fifties, was home with her two preschool-aged grandchildren. Although she was evasive in responding to my basic questions, such as "How many individuals live here?" and "Did you apply for compensation?" she still showed hospitality and served me tea. Once I informed her that the Amal Movement's representative had referred me to her, she willingly supplied the number of residents and told me about the future plans of her family. She reported that twenty-one relatives who belonged to four nuclear families had been registered as occupants of this apartment: Um Hussein herself, her married son, her married daughter, and her husband's brother and their families. Despite the clear contradiction in the empty, unused rooms around me, she matter-of-factly reported nearly two dozen home dwellers. Later on, she explained that although the four families did not permanently live there at the time of my visit, for the past twenty years they had lived there for various periods; hence, she believed they qualified for the compensation.

Initially, after the escalation of violence in 1976, Um Hussein, her husband, and her then-unmarried children had moved to this apartment after they were forced to flee their home in Borj Ḥammoud, in the Christian eastern part of the city. As was typical of wartime house-hunting, her oldest son secured this apartment after he had joined a prevailing militia in the area. After the war, the same son bought an apartment in the Southern Suburb of Beirut, while her brother-in-law returned to his ancestral village in South Lebanon. Despite owning two homes outside the city, the extended family continued to claim residence in the disputed apartment. To strengthen their claim of residency, in case they were visited by a representative of the Central Fund for the Displaced, the family decided to leave the two children with their grandmother. Um Hussein then explained the family's strategy of overreporting:

> Look at the poor condition of this place! Of course there is not enough room for all of us. Under normal conditions, humans could not live here! But during the war, we did not have any other choice; we all lived here. Now, after we learned that the compensation would be granted based on the size of the family, my son registered the four families as occupants of this apartment. The Amal Movement promised to get us the compensation money. We are still waiting. When we get the money, we will pay the whole amount as a down payment for a new apartment in the Southern Suburb. (Interview with Um Hussein, July 1997)

Um Hussein was aware that their claim was not strictly legitimate, but even her exaggerated claim rested on her family's prewar experiences, when she lived in crowded quarters in conditions she didn't consider fit for human beings. Though she didn't state it explicitly, she conveyed what others expressed directly: that the displaced believed that they were entitled to compensation for their wartime suffering, especially regarding their ordeals in relation to space. She also believed that the four families deserved the compensation because they lived in extreme poverty.

MULTILAYERED CORRUPTION

Solidere found it more cost-effective to pay compensation to the displaced rather than paying late fees to contractors, but state officials such as Kareem of the Central Fund for the Displaced strongly believed that Solidere's policies of overpaying the displaced had raised the expectations of other refugees. He further explained that when Solidere drafted its plans for the downtown area and signed agreements with contractors, it completely overlooked thousands of illegal residents who already occupied that area. Kareem also accused the displaced of exploiting the process and criticized Solidere for placing its priorities as a private investing firm over the interests and the well-being of the country and its residents.

Similarly, municipal officials accused the Hariri government of mishandling the funds allocated for the displaced. Randa, a municipality employee who processed many of the applications, believed that Prime Minister Hariri himself was engaged in an election scheme. She claimed that his nondisplaced supporters had received grants to renovate their homes from funds earmarked for the displaced. She then explained that in addition to the initial misdirecting of funds, the disbursement of the funds was manipulated by high officials at the municipality. It was stipulated that applicants needed to pay their overdue utility fees prior to being eligible to receive the grants. This prerequisite allowed the city to collect thousands of Lebanese liras without necessarily paying all the applicants. Because the funds were limited, the information about the new grants was not evenly disseminated, and the rules were changed midstream. Thus only a few residents were able to collect the home-repair money. Randa described the scheme:

> Three months before the elections, we received a memo instructing us to accept applications for home-repair grants from property owners. Although the grants were not publicly announced, Hariri supporters learned about them by word of mouth. We issued checks for the first few hundred applicants. By the time others learned about the funds, there was no money left, but we continued to accept their applications.

This account of irregular dissemination of information, manipulation of funds, unreliable processes, and political favoritism was characteristic of the postwar era. Randa recounted that when she questioned the scheme, her supervisor advised her to keep quiet and justified the process by saying that no one was harmed and both the municipality and Hariri benefited from this arrangement.

The political opposition raised similar doubts regarding the funds for the displaced. Najah Wakim, an outspoken parliament member representing the opposition, accused Hariri and the minister of the displaced of diverting 800 million U.S. dollars into unrelated projects such as building highways, developing a sports city, and making airport renovations. Wakim accused the government of drowning the country in unnecessary debt. He accused Hariri of accepting foreign aid and high-interest loans to resolve the displacement problem, which instead were used to execute his own private profitable projects (Wakim 1998, 122–123). This accusation contributed to the climate of rumors and uncertainty that also characterized the postwar era.

USING TIME AND SPACE TO ARGUE
THE CASE OF THE DISPLACED

The displaced themselves were then caught in a transitional stage, a state of "postwar emergency," because of the ambiguous messages they received from multiple sources, the corrupt dissemination of aid, and their exclusion from the future plans of the city. The displaced coped with this uncertainty by suppressing the present; doubting the future, as reflected in their frequent refrain "let's wait and see," which I heard from numerous interlocutors; claiming rootedness to the city; and asserting their right to space.

Faced with government-sponsored eviction, the displaced often called upon their wartime experiences to defend their rights to space. They stressed the length of their stay, "We lived in these places for over twenty years," and their emotional attachment to these sites, "We raised our children here." For many, the illegally occupied places may have been the only "home" they had ever known. During the war, the displaced claimed they had "purchased" their homes from other refugees on the black market, deals often brokered by militia members. Sacrificing their life savings and even their dowries to purchase these spaces solidified the feelings of belonging and claims to ownership.

To present themselves as loyal protectors of the city, the displaced evoked certain memories of the war. They stressed their continuous stay in Beirut and contrasted themselves to those who had abandoned their city "when it needed them the most," implying their own superior loyalty. The displaced used such past experiences to legitimize their presence and to defy the accusations of being illegal occupiers and a social burden.

Despite accusations and attempts at eviction, the displaced continued to present themselves as rightful residents who were emotionally attached to the homes where they had lived for over twenty years. Hence, they believed they had legitimate rights either to stay or to receive compensation. On the other hand, property owners, who might have left the country during the entire period of the war, could now return to reclaim their occupied properties. Claiming legitimacy became a key issue in the negotiations between the displaced and the landlords.

The displaced engaged in public discourse to define themselves and to legitimize their presence in the city. They argued that under the emergency circumstances of the war, and after they had lost their legal homes, it was justifiable to take over empty and abandoned buildings in safer areas. When they could not invoke legal financial contracts, many of them used economic and psychological metaphors: "We paid the price of these places with our lives, blood, and nerves." However, legal property owners enjoyed permanent legitimacy and had no need to invoke the past or to justify their wartime experiences.

When narrating their past experiences, the rural displaced constructed stories around specific sites, that is, their respective homes in Beirut. They often retraced the various refuge sites used over the past twenty years of war, and sometimes back to prewar places of residence. Um Mahmood, a Shi'ite woman in her seventies, first migrated to Beirut from the south when she got married in 1958. She had vivid memories of the six homes she occupied over the past three decades. She recalled the houses where she gave birth to her nine children, remembered the names of the landlords, told stories about her children playing or fighting with the neighbor's children, and specified the exact amount of money paid for rent.

Many of the displaced who had moved from the villages to the city often recalled their villages with nostalgic, pastoral qualities of intimate social relations. They spoke of large gatherings where relatives and neighbors helped each other in harvesting crops, building houses, and looking for stray animals. Despite this nostalgia, and although many maintained village connections or visited regularly, when the war ended, the majority of the displaced rejected the government's offer of returning them to their original homes. They declined for a number of reasons. First, the majority of the displaced in Beirut came from rural areas that lacked basic services and job opportunities. Second, because many of the displaced were Shi'ites from South Lebanon, it was impossible for them to return to their villages, since many of the villages were, at the time, still occupied by Israel.[13] In fact, the Israeli army was still forcing even more people to leave their homes. Third, the displaced, and especially their children who had lived most of their lives in Beirut, had adopted an urban lifestyle, making it unimaginable for them to return to their villages of origin. Additionally, a large number of displaced families were too traumatized to return to their places of origin, since many of them left their homes after experiencing massacres and threats. With these reasons in mind, the displaced invoked their belonging in the city, if not for their own sake, then for their offspring: "Our children are already urbanized. They know only Beirut as home." The displaced claimed rights to the city by arguing that a whole generation had been born and raised in the city, and their identities as well as their socioeconomic networks were shaped by its urban context.

The narratives of displacement I heard in my interviews expressed a different relation to time and space than the vision of reconstruction embodied by Solidere and government agencies, which suppressed memories of the war and viewed the future with optimism. Unlike many Beirutis, who associated wartime spaces and experiences with violence and horror, the displaced spoke favorably about the war. Their accounts described wartime as a stable period, citing the availability of economic resources, the chance to join political groups and parties, and, most important, their control over space in the city. Compared to the past, the present was mostly described as worse in terms of economic instability, lack of services, conflict among family members, and especially, the sense of being disoriented or lost, not knowing how to negotiate information, power, and resources.

SAHAR: THE POLITICS OF INFORMATION AND KNOWLEDGE

The case of Sahar, a forty-year-old mother of three, highlights the question of legitimacy about who has a right to own an apartment and who counts as "displaced." When I met Sahar in 1996, she was staying with her in-laws in Beirut. Having recently returned from three years in Saudi Arabia, she was locked out of the apartment she previously "owned," according to the unofficial real estate black market of the war era. Sahar's family was displaced at the beginning of the war when she was eight years old, when they were forced to move to 'Ayn el-Mreisse from East Beirut. She later married Ahmed, a displaced neighbor. The newly married couple was able to "buy" an apartment from another displaced family after Sahar had sold the gold she received as her dowry. They treated the space as if they enjoyed full ownership and responsibility: "We renovated it, replaced the windows, painted the walls, and connected the apartment to electricity from a neighboring generator."[14] After six years there, with the war still ongoing, they moved to Saudi Arabia for her husband's new job, but still considered the 'Ayn el-Mreisse apartment their permanent home: "While in Saudi Arabia, we kept all of our belongings in the apartment and left the key with my in-laws. We returned every year and spent the summer in our Beirut apartment."

Despite her emotional attachment to her apartment, Sahar was aware that the displaced who had taken over empty space during the war were soon to be evicted. Thus, when she heard about the compensation, Sahar asked her in-laws to submit an application on her behalf. But developers and landlords were already forcibly seizing occupied apartments with the state's sanction. Sahar got caught up in this process: "One day, we received a phone call from my in-laws informing us that the property owner had broken into our apartment and thrown our furniture and belongings out. I flew back to Beirut immediately," she said. The owner later claimed to have put an eviction notice under the door, as was legally required. According to him, Sahar and her family were illegal occupiers, yet Sahar considered the property her rightful possession or she believed that she at least merited compensation before she relinquished it. Without a formal legal contract to call on, she based her claim on her memories and experiences: She had paid for it with her dowry, renovated it, moved in as a new bride, and given birth there.

The eviction triggered not only a struggle for the apartment, but a contest over Sahar's status: could she be counted among the displaced? Officials at the Ministry of the Displaced informed Sahar and her husband, Ahmed, that they did not have the status of a "real displaced family." Although both of them had been uprooted while they were still children, they became ineligible to be considered a displaced family because they had left Lebanon. Nonetheless, Sahar contested the decision on the grounds that both her displacement and her marriage had occurred during the war, and she supported her argument with a list of people of similar background who had received compensation. (The people on her list, however, had not departed to live in another country as she had.) Later, she learned from the ministry that her three years in Saudi Arabia were the reason for her disqualification. Ironically, the original owner of "her" apartment had also spent fifteen years abroad, having lived in France throughout the war—but his travels did not affect his right to ownership as hers did. Sahar and her in-laws not only followed the postwar legal procedures in filing with the Ministry of the Displaced but also pursued informal political channels. Sahar was confident that the ministry refused her application because the original owner had access to influential people who enabled him to obtain the court-ordered eviction illegally.

The case of Sahar exemplifies how the interpretation of words such as "displaced" or "occupier," "legal" or "illegal," and "family" or "home" aroused great uncertainty in the daily lives of the refugees. Additionally, we also learn from Sahar's case what it meant to be simultaneously caught up in the intricate circles of bureaucracy and family conflicts. Sahar had to leave her husband and children in Saudi Arabia and return to Beirut to rescue her furniture and try to collect compensation. She had to prove her eligibility for compensation before the officials at the Ministry of the Displaced and the property owner. At the same time, she had to negotiate new relationships and a division of labor with her in-laws, who allowed her to stay, along with her children, whom she later brought to Beirut, in their small one-bedroom apartment. Her mother-in-law and one of the two sisters-in-law looked after her children during her interminable visits to the ministry. In return, the mother-in-law expected to receive some of the forthcoming compensation.

Sahar detailed her dilemma: "I do not know what to do with my furniture. Now it is all piled up on a balcony at my in-laws, exposed to the sun and humidity." She and her family were pushed into a liminal situation: "I cannot live with my in-laws for a long time. Their apartment is too small. In addition, they themselves have received an eviction notice. They do not know where they will end up." Sahar and her family were trapped in bureaucratic channels where they had to look for both formal and informal connections to gain access to governmental resources. Sahar was unable to return to her apartment, she was not sure she would receive compensation, she did not know how long she could stay with her in-laws, and she was not sure whether she could join her husband in Saudi Arabia.

ALI: RUNNING AROUND IN
POSTWAR BUREAUCRATIC CIRCLES

Notwithstanding the push toward postwar modernity, the division of functions among state institutions, developers, investors, and local religious and political groups was not at all clear. The overlap in responsibilities and personnel between the public and private sectors meant that a single individual could simultaneously hold a government position and own construction companies, like Hariri himself, without an outcry over conflict of interest. That individual, moreover, could easily have once been a militia commander who later became a political or religious leader and was still carrying those partisan affiliations with him.

This overlap in responsibilities and confusion about the bureaucratic process forced the displaced to "run around in circles" when they sought administrative help. This is what happened to Ali, a Shi'ite from South Lebanon, who had moved with his family to Beirut in 1979 when he was fifteen years old. During the war, he joined various political groups and militias, securing his family's daily needs with the help of militia leaders who controlled his neighborhood. Faced with eviction after the war, he was unsure how to proceed, which institution to contact in order to receive what he considered his due. I met Ali in the lull while he was waiting for his compensation from the Central Fund for the Displaced. He absorbed the general optimism of the aftermath of the war, since the reestablishment of the state had given the Lebanese population the hope that arbitrary systems of neighborhood strongmen and militias were now defunct. Based on this optimistic premise, Ali had filed his claim for compensation without the mediation of political or religious patrons.[15] "Now that there is a functioning legitimate state, we do not have to seek sectarian connections and alliances," he informed me.

Later, it became clear to Ali that the state's systems were not as transparent or as reliable as he initially expected. Ali encountered a number of obstacles:

When I heard about the compensation, I tried to file on my own. I went to the ministry several times. I stood in line for hours. Before seeing any of the officials at the ministry, I heard from other displaced that we had to collect signatures from the Central Fund for the Displaced, the *mukhtar*[16] of the village of origin, and the *mukhtar* of the neighborhood where we live now. I collected all the necessary documents and signatures and came back.

Ali's experience led him to realize that he had naively trusted the bureaucracy of the new state. He reported with cynicism:

When I made it to the official at the ministry, he asked me to go back for more documents and official signatures. They [state officials] would not pay attention to any application if it did not come through an influential person. Now we [the displaced] do not know the "rules of the new game," of how, where, and who can provide us with services and support.

Ali subsequently turned to the wartime militias that were being eclipsed by the state but still operated within it. He compared the wartime and postwar systems:

After the war, the logic of things changed. During the war, I used to seek the militia's help to find an apartment or a job. Now, yesterday's militia leaders have become today's politicians. Because they know that we are not dependent upon them as before, they are trying to keep us under their control. They want us to be like sheep that they own. They want us to realize that we cannot get anything done without their intervention.

Unfortunately, the government is afraid of the political and religious leaders; it listens to them but not to us. They are the government and the opposition at the same time. What can I tell you? If your enemy is the judge, to whom can you complain?

Ali had to resort to the methods used during the war, with their informal channels of information and rumors, in the absence of reliable official channels. Alarmed by rumors of a budget shortfall in the Ministry of the Displaced, Ali found an influential figure to intervene on his behalf. But that mediator's help was offered on condition of an unofficial exchange:

Finally, my cousin [who is also displaced] told me that he knew someone who was influential at the ministry and who could mediate on my behalf. The help was offered on the condition that I use the compensation money to buy an apartment in a housing project managed by the mediator and his brother.

Ali accepted his cousin's solution because he was not sure he would be able to win the compensation without help, especially after he heard rumors about the ministry's diminishing budget. Also, Ali and his family had to move from their neighborhood, where they had lived for seventeen years, to the Southern Suburb of Beirut. The compensation he received, Ali complained, "would not buy me a piece of a wall in this neighborhood," since it was under development by global capital investors for upper-end residences, businesses, and multinational establishments. Still, he considered himself lucky to be able to buy a two-bedroom apartment in a building in which "influential" people (*nas wasleen*)—the mediator and his brother—owned more than half the units. This ensured that should the government, ten years hence, decide to incorporate that area into its urban plans, he would be protected from yet another displacement.

Even with his influential connections, Ali was still not assured. A troublesome detail was that the mediator's new apartment building had yet to be built. The government compensation was only sufficient to pay the first installment on a dwelling he had so far only seen on a blueprint. Ali made provisional arrangements for the summer, but expressed anxiety about the near future:

> Now that it is summertime, I sent my wife and children to stay with my mother in the village. I am staying temporarily with friends and relatives in Beirut. Sometimes, I sleep at construction sites and get paid as a night guard. The serious problems will start when school begins [in the fall]. Who is going to host my three children in the city? I do not want to think about it right now!

Although Ali had exhausted his connections with family, friends, and politicians, he continued to face a predicament. He did not have a permanent place in the city, he was not sure if his children would be able to return to their school, and, finally, he was not sure when the apartment he bought would be ready for him to move in.

Ali's case illustrates how intricately formal systems were interlaced with the informal systems of quid pro quo contracts that evolved directly from wartime practices. Ali's story is a microcosm of the complex negotiations for housing in postwar Beirut. Most of the war-displaced were unsure how much money they would be paid, when they would receive it, or where to go after being evicted from their wartime niches. To obtain what was owed to them, they often had to obligate themselves to others — relatives and political patrons — and these social duties undermined their ability to plan, creating more uncertainty in the present and unpredictability for the future. Each dilemma enmeshed them in a multilayered web in which the state, the politicians, and their kin were all entangled.

The Lebanese state and its institutions (the Ministry of the Displaced, the Central Fund for the Displaced), as well as private developers such as Solidere (supported by Hariri's company and entwined with the government, as explained in Chapter Two), were all violating the rights of the displaced to a decent home, privacy, and reputation, according to the Universal Declaration of Human Rights. Article 12 invokes living space as a basic human entitlement:

> No one shall be subjected to arbitrary interference with his privacy, family, home or correspondence, nor to attack upon his honour and reputation. Everyone has the right to the protection of the law against such interference or attacks. (United Nations 1948)

The rights of the displaced were denied based on the fact that they were not given homes, their family lives were interrupted, and their reputations were attacked. The unjust policies toward the displaced exacerbated the postwar chaos, perpetuating a state of emergency even after the violence had ended. These policies in effect caused further displacement. As a developmental scheme, Solidere's reconstruction project caused further dislocation of people by forcing the war-displaced to evacuate occupied properties, displacing even some of the legal tenants and owners, not only in downtown Beirut but in other surrounding areas.

The new government implemented its policies and endorsed the efforts of Solidere (with which it was entwined) in the name of development, reconstruction, modernity, and reconciliation. For Solidere and the postwar government, development and modernity meant creating a cosmopolitan global city, in the hope of attracting investors and tourists, but at the same time it excluded its vulnerable residents from its future urban plans. The policies toward the displaced aimed at evacuating them from areas close to central Beirut but did not offer a long-term plan of finding alternative housing for hundreds of thousands of the city's residents.

CONCLUDING REMARKS

Despite their marginalization from the reconstruction agendas, the war-displaced used various strategies to negotiate for their rights to housing—staying in the same homes, finding alternative homes in other areas, or receiving compensation for being evicted from the illegally occupied properties.

The cases of the displaced families presented in this chapter demonstrate that this population continued to live in a state of liminality. The uncertainty in their lives had intensified even further in the aftermath of the war.

Although the media, developers, politicians, and the nondisplaced Beirutis all viewed the displaced as reminders of the war and a threat to the presumed postwar stability, this disadvantaged group created both temporary and permanent alliances to pressure politicians to advocate on their behalf. In their negotiations for homes and cash compensation, the displaced used their attachment to space to lay claim to the homes they occupied. They recalled personal experiences, their wartime resilience and sacrifices, and their many years of living in squatter areas to place pressure on developers and government institutions (the Ministry of the Displaced and the Central Fund for the Displaced) to grant them the compensation they believed they deserved.

The failure of the reconstruction project to incorporate the needs of this marginal group, and the socioeconomic ruptures created by top-down planning, caused more uncertainty and dislocated the displaced one more time, forcing them to create new squatter areas on the outskirts of Beirut. Thus the reconstruction project reproduced the very symptoms it was designed to eliminate.

Although the rebuilding of Beirut's Central District has been completed, life in the city has not returned to normal. The recent turmoil that resulted from the assassination of Prime Minister Rafik Hariri in February 2005,[1] the Cedar Revolution in March 2005, the withdrawal of Syrian troops from Lebanon in April 2005, and the Israeli bombing of Beirut in July 2006 had escalated the "state of emergency" and placed the country on the verge of yet another conflict.

The assassination of former prime minister Hariri under murky circumstances on February 14, 2005, had tumbled the already fragile Lebanese political structure. Hariri's death sparked the so-called Cedar Revolution, a conflict in which political clashes occurred between the supporters of the government and the opposition. Thousands demonstrated in the downtown district, starting a chain reaction that led to the withdrawal of the Syrian military from Lebanon and, ultimately, a war between Israel and Hizballah in July 2006. These dramatic events can be traced to the competition over the control of space and the claim to the nation's contested past, themes discussed in earlier chapters.

In what follows I examine the ways in which political and economic instability changed the symbolic and functional meaning of Beirut's Central District. The significance of the downtown area in the imagination of Beirutis can be traced through its various popular names. Before and during the civil war, city residents continued to call it the "Center of the Country" (*wast al-balad*). Later, during the reconstruction era, many referred to it as "the Solidere." After it was rebuilt, however, the wealthy Lebanese and the tourists who frequented its luxurious facilities named it the English word "al-dawntawn" or just "al-DT." But after the recent political turmoil, its name has changed one more time. When protestors of all ages and from all socioeconomic and political backgrounds took over its streets, built tents, and camped there for months, the area came to be called "Al-Najmeh Square" (Saḥat al-Najmeh), or just "the Square" (al-Saḥa).

The symbolic significance of this Central District is not limited to its ever-changing name. Political groups paraded their power and influence by filling the square with thousands of their followers. After Rafik Hariri was buried in the historic Martyrs' Square, his grave became a "shrine" and a site of public protest.[2] On March 14, 2005, a month after his death, thousands gathered there and renamed the area "Freedom Square." More than four hundred young men and women wearing white-and-red scarves and carrying the Lebanese flag, symbols of the Hariri coalition, erected tents and camped out in the downtown area day and night. They demanded the withdrawal of the Syrian army from Lebanon and called upon the international community to investigate the death of Hariri. Later, a political group emerged, calling itself the March 14th Coalition or the Future Coalition.

The space became further contested when antigovernment protesters, led by the Shi'ite political party Hizballah and the Maronite Christian leader Michel Aoun, occupied the area, marking it with their yellow-and-orange flags. It was estimated by the Hizballah-run Al-Manar TV station that more than a million and a half individuals flocked to the area on December 1, 2006.[3] Similar to the March 14th Coalition, the Hizballah followers also staged their own sit-in, with tents stretching from Hariri's gravesite to the upper part of Martyrs' Square and Riad Solh Street. The protesters vowed that their occupation would last until the government of Prime Minister Fouad Siniora was overthrown. To protect it from violent attacks, the gravesite was guarded by army personnel and sealed off with barbed razor wire. The crowds were described as "eclectic, from sober-looking clerics in traditional robes to supporters of Aoun who had dyed their hair [with the group's trademark] orange. Others had donned orange wigs and cowboy hats. Some of the slogans were sectarian, [but] at times, though, the crowd aimed for [nonsectarian] chants with broader appeal" (Shadid 2006, A01).

The government-supported Future Coalition and the Hizballah-led opposition asserted their influence, calling upon followers to assemble in the contested downtown area. The continued struggle over the Martyrs' Square/Freedom Square exploded on March 14, 2006, a year and a month after Hariri's assassination. While the opposition continued its sit-in at Martyrs' Square, Saad Hariri, the heir of the deceased prime minister and the new leader of the pro-government coalition, called on his supporters to commemorate his father with a massive turnout at the leader's gravesite. The atmosphere was somber, schools and shops were closed for the day, and politicians were forced to observe a moment of silence and give their speeches from behind bulletproof glass screens. The speakers called for national unity, accused the Syrian regime of assassinating members of the Future Coalition, and commemorated the slain prime minister. In his speech, Saad Hariri accused the opposition of terrorism and of taking over Beirut. Michael Slackman, a *New York Times* journalist, stated that "the anniversary offered the government one day, at least, to take control of the city from the opposition supporters on the other side of the razor wire" (Slackman 2007). With tensions rising, both parties agreed that the army needed to be brought in to prevent violent confrontations.

Both the government's coalition and the opposition claimed that they represented an oppressed majority and accused each other of provoking sectarian rivalry, working for foreign powers, and "trading in the blood of martyrs." These accusations were disseminated through "the battle of billboards" and through the media. Government supporters plastered Beirut with large portraits of Rafik Hariri and his son Saad and with bright red posters that read "WE LOVE LIFE." The opposition, for their part, responded with posters declaiming fervently "WE WANT TO LIVE . . . WITH DIGNITY" and flew the yellow-and-green Hizballah flag (Khouri 2007).

In addition to jockeying for power through the physical occupation of Beirut's downtown and the posting of billboards, the warring parties took their conflict to cyberspace. This new medium allowed the factions to debate political views, circulate their messages to a wider global audience, and recruit supporters for their large protests. It is widely reported and quite apparent that these young demonstrators were media savvy and experts at constructing the image they wanted to portray.

Viewing Internet video youtube.com postings, it became abundantly clear that the activists were fully aware of the presence of the video camera and that they were performing for a global audience. Many of them spoke in English and provided historical facts for non-Lebanese viewers.[4] On the local level, a large number of the protestors stated that prior to the sit-in they had never participated in this type of political action, but admitted that after receiving electronic messages from friends they had been moved to join in the struggle.

This electronic news media was masterfully exploited by the protesters to great effect during the thirty-three-day Israeli invasion of Lebanon, an event that changed the balance of power between the warring groups. On July 12, 2006, the Israeli army launched a massive attack on Lebanon after Hizballah kidnapped two Israeli soldiers with the intention of exchanging them for Lebanese prisoners held in Israel.[5]

Lebanese bloggers and "media activists" responded to these attacks through cyberspace. Pictures of destroyed bridges, bombed-out buildings, burned ambulances, and children buried under rubble, as well as aerial images before and after the bombing, were widely distributed.[6] For example, a cyber activist group known as Electronic Lebanon provided daily commentaries, political analysis, human rights reports, and voices from the ground. Some Web sites offered hour-by-hour coverage, while others raised funds to feed and house the thousands who were displaced by this act of aggression. A group called the Civil Resistance Campaign was formed to create alliances with local and international grassroots organizations. This group's Web site[7] provided news coverage of the war, a collection of photos, and links to related Web sites; they even designed posters that could be printed in any size for use in demonstrations.

This easy access to electronic media enabled many alternative voices to be heard. Despite the fact that they were ignored by the majority of traditional media,[8] this new cyberspace phenomenon attracted the attention of international mainstream media outlets. CNN accused media activists of distorting the facts and of "doctoring their electronic images." Amer Saidi, a blogger, countered these attacks and accused the network of bias, because he found that it did not reveal that "the Israeli government was actually paying Israeli Web surfers to monitor Lebanese blogs and write responses favorable to Israel."[9] Unlike CNN, the BBC incorporated material provided by these bloggers into their coverage. The network hosted a debate between two bloggers,[10] Rania Masri from Lebanon and Lisa Goldman from Israel, and asked them to respond to the following question: "With both the Israeli government and Hezballah claiming victory in the month-long conflict, . . . who [do] you think won the war?" The two bloggers debated the cause of the war heatedly and discussed its impact on their communities, while viewers posted supporting and opposing remarks.

While these battles were being fought in cyberspace, activists also succeeded in exacting change in Beirut's physical landscape. As a result of their large-scale demonstrations and sit-ins, the supporters of the government and the opposition were able to economically cripple the newly renovated Central District. Their constant presence kept customers away and forced businesses to close down or move to other locations. Ironically, the economic "death" of the downtown area unwittingly revived the Hamra Street market, in a neighborhood that had suffered economically after the recovery of the business district. The success of Taʾ-Marbouta, a recently launched café frequented by young media activists, is an example of an urban site that emerged to satisfy the changing needs of its customers.

Bilal, one of the co-owners of the café, told me his motivation for opening the café:

> When I moved back to Beirut in 2005 after living in New York for many years, I worked with indie media activists about issues related to Iraq and Palestine and later with Lebanese politics. Many of these activists used to gather at the old Modca Café. After the closure of Modca, there was a dire need for a place to meet and socialize. (From an interview carried out in July 2007)

Bilal and his partner chose the Hamra area as a location for their new café. After a few months of searching for just the right place, they settled on an abandoned restaurant occupying the first floor of a run-down hotel. Initially worried that the reputation of the residents of the hotel (who happened to be sex workers) might keep customers away, they found that their café was a great success. Desirous of an "authentic atmosphere," they chose an Arabic name, rather than following the customary habit of adopting a Western name. Bilal explained the reason for choosing a single letter of the Arabic alphabet, Ta'-Marbouta, as a name: "We asked our friends to come up with suggestions. . . . Finally, we decided that a letter, Ta'-Marbouta, would work. It makes a nice logo, it is unusual, and, more importantly, it cannot be translated into English." Striving for more authenticity, they also bought the furniture from local merchants. After six months of renovation, the café was scheduled to open on July 18, 2006, but ironically that date turned out to be six days after the most recent Israeli attack on Beirut. "On July 12, the day of the invasion, I was sending out e-mail invitations for the opening," Bilal commented sarcastically.

The 2006 war dictated the kind of "regulars" this café attracted, as well as molding its character and reputation. Accustomed to sporadic Israeli attacks, at first the owners did not expect that the bombing would last for the whole month. But when the war atrocities increased, the opening had to be canceled. The contractors, who had neglected to complete the work prior to the conflict, unexpectedly arrived to finish the job and to collect their pay for fear of losing their contracts. Despite the war, all renovations were completed, the kitchen was ready, and a chef was hired.

The owners, politically involved themselves, joined other activists who had rechanneled their activities from the sit-ins in the downtown area to efforts to provide emergency aid for the refugees squatting in the Sannaye

Garden and in public schools. When members of the various nongovernmental organizations and political groups[11] needed a place to coordinate their relief efforts, Bilal and his partner offered their newly renovated café. And the chef, who had previously lived in Beirut's Southern Suburb, an area badly hit by Israeli rockets, now found refuge in the hotel above the café. Using donated supplies, he began his work at the café by cooking one thousand meals every day, which were then hauled in a huge pot to feed the refugees. Ta'-Marbouta Café thus became the de-facto headquarters for groups who fed the displaced, distributed hygiene kits, collected donations, and offered help to traumatized children. To get their message out, the activists also took it upon themselves to install a wireless connection through which to broadcast their reports on cyberspace.

One week into the war, Bilal left Beirut and joined war correspondents reporting from the war zone in South Lebanon. Upon his return to Beirut, he was happily surprised at the large number of volunteers who congregated at the café. He described the café as "completely full. There were at least three groups holding meetings at the same time; one sat on couches, a second gathered around the two large tables in the back, while refugee children received counseling in the library room." The clientele consisted mainly of "young women and men in their twenties and thirties who yearned for a café with a social conscience."

Despite the cancellation of its official opening, when the war finally ended, Ta'-Marbouta was already a functioning café—but without revenue. Bilal commented, "We found ourselves in a strange bind. We wanted a transition from offering free drinks to the volunteers who became our friends to functioning as a profitable business." A diplomatic solution was reached. Not wanting to offend the volunteers, the waiters discreetly distributed menus, took orders, and expected payment. The official opening finally took place two weeks later.

Now, the café has established its own loyal clientele of young activists, artists, and journalists. The owners were pleased with their customers and decided not to do further advertising. Bilal explained their strategy: "We did not want some random tourists or the downtown cookie crowd coming in. . . . We didn't want to function as a pure business, but at the same time we do not want to go under."

Amenities and activities were added to further the mission of the café. An additional room was transformed into a library where the owners made available their own books as well as ones that were donated and purchased for the customers to borrow. This room was also offered free of charge for community meetings. An event coordinator was also hired. Singers and musicians were invited to perform, and a tradition of a weekly open-mike night was established to encourage emerging artists. Ta'-Marbouta was also the first café in Beirut to offer free wireless connection, a service that was later offered by neighboring competitors. The work of visual artists was displayed and sold, and independent films rarely found in mainstream theaters were screened.

The volunteers, who were primarily college students, often returned to the café with new projects. Sociology students, for example, began to invite speakers to their monthly "Sociology Café." Students from the Department of Agriculture at American University of Beirut sold "Healthy Baskets" on behalf of local peasant women. Three architectural students involved in the rebuilding of Ayata Ashaab, a destroyed village in the south, presented their architectural plans at the café and even invited the mayor of the village to their presentation.

CONCLUDING REMARKS

The completion of Solidere's project at the end of the last century did not bring an end to the "state of emergency." Years after my fieldwork, 2005–2006 saw dramatic events: the assassination of Prime Minister Hariri (who spearheaded the reconstruction efforts), the unexpected withdrawal of the Syrian army from Lebanon, and the Israeli bombing of Beirut. These onslaughts left the country in political mayhem. The newly revived downtown area, initially designed for peaceful commingling, now became a hub where opposing factions took their fights. To assert their political influence, political rivals assembled tens of thousands of protesters who transformed the glossy downtown into a "tent city," which obstructed the regular commerce and thereby undermined the area's economy.

The activists' transformation of the city highlighted enormous contrasts between private and public, elite and other classes, polished or improvised. After the downtown's upscale private amenities had been shaped to serve the country's elite, public streets were taken over by a younger generation that crossed economic classes (and who had come of age during the civil war). Although excluded from the initial reconstruction, the demonstrators succeeded in inserting themselves centrally in this space, and they used their takeover to voice political demands. When protestors camped with tents in streets and public squares for months, they transformed these spaces into semiprivate sites.

The political unrest, the foreign interference, and the Israeli destruction of infrastructure pushed Lebanon to the verge of yet another civil war, a worry that magnified the long-running climate of uncertainty. Despite the unpredictability of the present, the activists formed groups that fought for various rights, some of which were spatial. The case of Ta'-Marbouta Café exemplifies a social site that, though established for another purpose, came to serve the needs of the emerging groups.

In addition to the competition over the downtown, activists now fought against each other in a new kind of space, cyberspace. They used Web sites, blogs, and e-mail to meet, fund-raise, disseminate information, represent their movements visually, recruit, and organize.

Even as they worked with very new media, the young activists also relied on a vision of the past, similar to the strategies of the individuals and groups discussed in earlier chapters. In a new turn, however, the past invoked by the activists now included some of the origins of the problems that colored Beirut, notably the former prime minister Hariri. In the aftermath of the war, he had been instrumental in launching the upscale reconstruction oriented toward global capital; once assassinated, however, he was absorbed in nostalgic homage, becoming part of the lost glory of the city.

NOTES

INTRODUCTION

1. The word "Solidere" is an acronym for the French term "Société libanaise pour le développement et la reconstruction Centre Ville du Beyrouth," which means "The Lebanese Company for the Development and Reconstruction of the Beirut Central District." Prime Minister Rafik Hariri (killed by a car bomb in February 2005) was a shareholder and a strong supporter of the company's plans. The company's role and politics will be discussed in Chapter Two.

2. The Ministry of the Displaced asked the displaced families to register their names to receive compensation for evacuating the buildings where they lived during the war. The government's policies toward the displaced population will be discussed in Chapter Six.

CHAPTER ONE

1. I visited Beirut for the first time in the summer of 1995 to conduct preliminary research about the rebuilding of postwar Beirut. I returned to Beirut in 1996 and 1997, living in the city for a total of over eighteen months.

2. After Solidere demolished many buildings in the downtown area, archaeologists were able to conduct salvage excavations.

3. In Brazil and Egypt, local governments used space as a symbol of modernity to justify carrying out major projects to restructure urban space and to assert their power.

4. The Green Line ran through the downtown area, dividing it into two. Areas surrounding the dividing line became strategic locations and battlefields for militias that changed throughout the war.

5. A number of anthropologists wrote about the politics of conducting field research among their own communities and discussed the role of the so-called native/indigenous anthropologist. See Abu-Lughod (1991), Altorki and El-Solh (1988), Jones (1995), Narayan (1993), and Paerregaard (2002).

6. The few Palestinians who were able to acquire Lebanese citizenship often concealed their identity. For an excellent analysis of the conditions of Palestinians in Lebanon, see Sayigh (1994) and Peteet (1996, 1997, 2005).

7. See King and Scheid 2006 for information about the anthropology in Lebanon.

8. Altorki and El-Solh (1988), *Arab Women in the Field: Studying Your Own Society*, is the first published book about the experiences of Arab women anthropologists.

9. Baydoun (1999), Gilsenan (1996), Machnouk (1994). For a thorough critique about using statistics in social sciences, see Asad (1994).

10. In Arabic, the word *balad* means "country." Before the war and immediately in its aftermath, residents of Beirut continued to call the downtown area the city center (*wasaṭ al-balad*). *Wasaṭ al-balad* literally means "the center of the country."

11. Initially, I believed that the speakers were talking about the building that accommodated the offices of Solidere. In the early phase of the reconstruction project, Solidere renovated one building in the midst of the war-torn central district that housed its offices.

CHAPTER TWO

1. During the war, secular, revolutionary, and nonreligious parties found themselves operating in a way similar to that of sectarian war militias. Although nonsectarian parties adopted secular ideologies, these parties were associated with the sectarian background of their leaders. For example, the Progressive Socialist Party, with its charismatic leader Kamal Jumblat, was seen as a Druze party. For a discussion about the role of sectarianism in Lebanese political groups, see Abu-Khalil (1985) and Dagher (2000).

2. Rafik Hariri became the prime minister in 1992 and was reelected in 2000. He resigned in October 2004 to protest Syria's intervention to extend the presidency of Emile Lahoud for three more years. Hariri was killed on February 14, 2005, by a car bomb (Fisk 2005).

3. In his study "The Genesis of a Mosque: Negotiating Sacred Space in Downtown Beirut," Ward Vloeberghs (2008) presents the conflict of interest between developers, archaeologists, and historians of ancient Beirut.

4. *Madina* is the Arabic feminine word that means "city." In Arabic literature, the city is often referred to by the feminine pronoun.

5. Before the war, the Orient building housed a major theater and various offices and shops.

6. The Tabula Rasa method is one where the city center is completely demolished and rebuilt with a new design (Davey 2000).

7. It is important to note that in most of these accounts, periods of decay were presented as a deviation from the normal state, even though some of these periods lasted longer than peaceful times.

8. Rafik Hariri's city of origin is Sidon (Sayda), located south of Beirut.

9. For scholarly works about the history of Lebanon during the Ottoman period, see Akarli (1993), Fawaz (1994), U. Makdisi (2000), and Salibi (1988).

10. The *mukhtar* is the neighborhood local leader officially appointed by the state.

11. In the postwar era of reconstruction, the red-tiled houses were considered the traditional Beiruti houses that were worth preserving. There were various calls to restore them to preserve the city's endangered heritage and identity.

12. For a recent and thorough study of Ottoman Beirut, see Hanssen (2005).

13. Shiber, quoted in Tabet (1993, 85).

14. Sociological writings blamed the newcomers for causing urban chaos because of their lack of "urban culture." Samir Khalaf and Guilian Denoeux argued that urbanism did not become a way of life in prewar Beirut because rural immigrants kept their traditional informal networks that were based on kinship and sectarian affiliations (1988, 181).

15. Camille Chamoun served as the president of Lebanon during the years 1952–1958. For more details about the Chamoun plans for Beirut, see Labaki (1993).

16. In a conference paper entitled "The Emerging Trends in Urbanism: The Beirut Postwar Experience," Robert Saliba (2000) mapped out the government's various plans to rebuild downtown Beirut.

17. It is estimated that one quarter of all dwelling units nationwide were damaged or demolished and half of the population was temporarily or permanently displaced from their homes (Charif 1994; Faour 1991; Trendle 1991). The country's total population is estimated at 3.5 million. After the war, more than half of the Lebanese population lives in Beirut.

18. A *fatwa* is a religious decree issued by a number of Muslim scholars regarding a disputed legal matter.

19. Interview with the leader of the Islamic Group in April 1997.

20. Interview with Jad Tabet in June 1997.

21. I interviewed Issam Noman two days after he had lost the 1996 election.

22. Beirut's Annual Arabic Book Exhibit was an annual tradition before the war. It was a major regional function that attracted intellectuals from neighboring Arab countries. The exhibit was halted during the years of conflict.

CHAPTER THREE

1. The *sarvees* is a four-passenger Mercedes car that drives through the streets of Beirut without a designated route. Passengers stop the *sarvees* and inform the driver of their destination. Based on the route of the passengers who are present in the car, the driver decides to take an extra one or two passengers. The new passenger negotiates a single or a double fare. The same *sarvees* functions as a taxi, with a single passenger paying the equivalent of four fares.

2. The phrases "oil money" and "Gulf dollars" are often used to refer to investors from the Gulf states such as Saudi Arabia, United Arab Emirates, and Qatar or to Lebanese citizens who worked in these countries and invested in real estate and postwar reconstruction. Similarly, "money from Africa" refers to the remittances sent mostly by Shi'ites who immigrated to French-speaking West African countries.

3. For more details on the history of the "traditional Beiruti houses," see Haddad (1999), Makhzoumi and Zako (2007), and Ragette (1980). APSAD (Association for Protecting Natural Sites and Old Buildings in Lebanon) is an example of nongovernmental organizations that work on preserving some of the remaining traditional Beiruti houses.

4. For more details on the role of Syria in Lebanon, see S. Haddad (2002), Norton (2000), and Saghieh (2005).

5. Acquaintances exchanged stories about the suffering and humiliations they experienced at Syrian-controlled checkpoints during and after the war.

6. In 2000, an investor renovated the House of the Lebanese Craftsman, and it became an upscale restaurant overlooking the Mediterranean.

7. In 1997, the Municipality of Beirut granted property owners a limited time to pay fees in order to obtain licenses for illegal buildings constructed during the war. Many property owners built illegal additions to existing structures and planned on paying fines.

8. During the war, local entrepreneurs ran privately owned generators and sold electricity to their neighbors.

9. For an excellent study about the commemoration of 'Ashura' in the Southern Suburb of Beirut, see Deeb (2005).

10. The work of Mona Harb (2001) is an excellent example of the alliances between wartime militia leaders and postwar investors in another part of Beirut.

11. It is important to note that during the war the number of Shi'ite residents of the neighborhood had increased dramatically. However, many of the original residents, Sunni Muslims and Druze, continued to reside in the area during and after the war.

12. I am aware that my definition of the area is also a construction. After living in two apartments on different streets in the neighborhood during my eighteen-month fieldwork, I found that the borders of the area changed according to the opinions of the people I interviewed and with whom I socialized.

13. In the 1996 parliamentary elections, eighteen ethnoreligious groups were recognized in Lebanon. The representation for each sectarian group in the parliamentary seats is based on the official size of the groups as well as their political power on the national level. The space here does not permit a discussion of the historical and contemporary formation of these groups, but for an overview, see Salibi (1988) and Nassar (1995).

14. During the war, and because of the area's proximity to the city center and the Green Line, militias competed for control of the neighborhood. With the

complete absence of the state, area residents were forced to seek sectarian alliances to acquire the necessary services. The sectarian affiliations fluctuated over the sixteen years of war. Many Beirutis switched their political alliances based on the militias in charge of their area. No single sectarian group or militia was able to control the same space in ʿAyn el-Mreisse all the time. Sometimes members who belonged to the same religious group fought each other. Alongside sectarian groups, nonreligious, or secular, parties and militias existed, yet most of them were identified with religious or ethnic groups. For example, the Progressive Socialist Party (Al-Ḥizb al-Taqadumī al-Ishtiraki) was known as a Druze party, and an Arab nationalist group named Al-Murabiṭoun was associated with the Sunni Muslims. For more details on the history of the political groups and their connections to sectarianism, see Fisk (1990), Traboulsi (1994), and Traboulsi (2007).

15. Interview with Ahmad, a resident of ʿAyn el-Mreisse.

16. Chapter Five provides a detailed analysis of displacement.

CHAPTER FOUR

1. Michael Davie (1987) reports that maps from 1840 showed that ʿAyn el-Mreisse was used as a fishing port as far back as that date.

2. Abu ʿAdnan al-Sayyad is his real name. Unlike my practice for the majority of my other interlocutors, I did not change his name because he is the only chief of the fishermen in ʿAyn el-Mreisse. Also, he wanted me to use his real name in the hope that the voice of the fishermen would be heard.

3. In the aftermath of the war, many nongovernmental organizations were established with the primary purpose of protecting certain aspects of the past. The following are examples of these organizations: the Association for Memory and Development (AMED), which aims to preserve the built and natural heritage; the Association for the Safeguarding of Sites and Old Residences (APSAD), which seeks to raise awareness about environmental problems and to encourage the safekeeping of the cultural and natural heritage of the country (later on, APSAD added another dimension to its mission, which is the safeguarding of old constructions. It also promoted the annual Daraj el-Fann exhibition in the Gemayze area and produced postcards depicting Beirut's old houses); the Audi Foundation, aimed at rediscovering the heritage of the city, revalorizing tourism, organizing artistic and cultural activities (exhibitions, conferences, seminars, concerts), and promoting the revival of traditional professions; the Cultural Dialogue Circle, which worked for the promotion of heritage and popular education; and other organizations such as the National Foundation for Heritage and the Beirut Heritage Association.

4. A number of Arab scholars have debated issues of heritage, authenticity, and modernity. For further information, see al-ʿAzmeh (1987), Rifai (2001), and Tarabishi (1991, 1993, 2000).

1. For a list of novels, memoirs, and films that addressed the war, see Chapter Two.

2. In the past few years, a number of feminist writings have reexamined the public/private dichotomy. For example, Elizabeth Thompson (2003) called for a direct interrogation of these terms.

3. For more details about the exclusively male traditional coffeehouses, see Amjad Nasir (1996). Shawqi Dwayhi's (2005) book, *Beirut's Popular Coffeehouses 1950–1990* (*Maqahi Beirut al-Shabeya 1950–1990*), is an excellent sociological study of the different kinds of coffeehouses that existed in Beirut before and during the civil war.

4. For information about the history of the Modca Café and its role in the lives of intellectuals, see Saqr Abu Fakhir (2002).

5. For a detailed description of the Hamra District during the 1960s–1970s, see Khalaf and Kongstad (1973).

6. Regional and local circumstances contributed to making Beirut a "cosmopolitan" city and a financial and cultural center for the Arab world. During the 1950s, a large number of Palestinian, Syrian, and Egyptian bourgeoisie were forced out of their countries and found refuge for themselves and their investments in Beirut. The occupation of Palestine and the establishment of Israel and the nationalization of resources by socialist governments in neighboring Syria and Egypt, combined with the flexible financial laws in Lebanon, allowed Beirut to become the major financial center in the region. Later on, Beirut's banks and financial institutions served the vast, growing oil markets of the Arabian Gulf region.

7. *Signs: A Special Issue on Gender and Cultural Memory* 28 (2002): 1.

8. Many women took part in the Lebanese civil war. The majority of them provided needed services to their communities or formed local groups, and some joined militias and political groups. Despite this participation, there are few writings devoted to women's role in the war. The following are examples of the writings about women and the Lebanese civil war: Accad (1989, 1990); Bryce et al. (1989) Cooke (1988, 1997); Shehadeh (1999); Sibai, Fletcher, and Armenian (2001).

9. Stories of women crossing checkpoints can be found in Miriam Cooke's two books, *War's Other Voices: Women Writers on the Lebanese Civil War* (1988) and *Women and the War Story* (1997). Also, Etel Adnan's novel *Sitt Marie Rose* revolves around the protagonist's experiences of crossing the infamous Green Line.

10. The militias changed over time, but in many cases, the same individual simply transferred from one militia to the other. For a detailed description about the various wartime militias, see Robert Fisk, *Pity the Nation* (1990).

11. It is important to note that Dwayhi did not include the "French"-style cafés in his description of the coffee-drinking venues in Beirut.

12. The *ḥusayniyah* is a place of gathering where Shiʿite religious rituals are performed.

13. In Lebanon, there are many maids from Sri Lanka, the Philippines, and India. Because of the dominant presence of maids from Sri Lanka, many Lebanese refer to all maids as Sri Lankan, regardless of their national origin. When Omar referred to customers who were accompanied by maids and dogs, he meant the upper class of the city. For additional information about the conditions of the domestic servants in Lebanon, see Bou-Habib (1998) and Jureidini and Moukarbel (2004).

CHAPTER SIX

1. For more details on prewar rural-urban migration in Lebanon, see Fuad Khuri's *From Village to Suburb: Order and Change in Beirut* (1975).

2. Thousands of Lebanese were forced out of their villages as a result of the continuous Israeli bombing and occupation of South Lebanon. Part of South Lebanon was occupied by Israel until 2000. In July 2006, Israel attacked South Lebanon and other parts of the country, forcing eighty thousand Lebanese to become war refugees.

3. The Amal Movement and the Hizballah Party were the two major Shiʿite Muslim political groups in West Beirut competing to represent the Shiʿite displaced population in their negotiations for compensation from the government and from the owners of properties occupied by the displaced.

4. The displaced in Lebanon belonged to various ethnoreligious groups: Christian Maronite, Greek Orthodox Christian, Sunni Muslim, Shiʿite Muslim, and Druze. In this chapter, I focus on the situation of the displaced Shiʿites.

5. Interview with an official at the Ministry of the Displaced.

6. Although Palestinians who lived in refugee camps in Beirut were displaced during the Lebanese civil war (1975–1991), they were excluded from the ministry's compensation programs for the displaced.

7. The Ministry of the Displaced used the family as a unit to estimate the number of the displaced, without giving a specific definition of the "family." During the war and after, many relatives joined households of their kin temporarily or permanently.

8. Interview with Khalil Abu Rjeileh on May 29, 1997, Beirut.

9. Ibid. For example, the minister of the displaced, Walid Jumblat, was the leader of the Druze militia (the Progressive Socialist Party). Many Christians accuse the Druze militia of having forced the Maronite Christians out of their villages in the region of Mount Lebanon.

10. Here the official at the Central Fund for the Displaced is being sarcastic. The phrase "breathing fresh air" (*sham hawa*) is used to indirectly refer to those who moved from the villages and the mountains to Beirut seeking entertainment and luxurious services that they lacked in their villages of origin.

11. Interview with an official at the Ministry of the Displaced in 1997.

12. In the process of evacuation, political parties, mostly Hizballah and the Amal Movement, presented themselves as defendants and representatives of the displaced.

13. The Israeli army withdrew from large areas of South Lebanon in 2000.

14. Until 1998, the state did not provide electricity to all residential areas. It was the responsibility of each house to provide its own. Enterprising people bought generators and sold electricity to their neighbors, charging them on a monthly or weekly basis.

15. For more details on patron-client relationships in Beirut, see Johnson (1986).

16. The *mukhtar* is a neighborhood-level or village-based authority, appointed by the state, who is responsible for registering births and deaths and issuing proof of residence.

AFTERWORD

1. For more details about the consequences of Hariri's sudden death, see Blanford (2006).

2. The public protest that was called "the Lebanese Intifada" by the Lebanese government was described by the U.S. media as "the Cedar Revolution."

3. This number was limited to tens of thousands when reported by the Hariri-owned Future TV station.

4. For more information, see the following links: http://www.youtube.com/watch?v=8iU8qSkm6zs; http://www.youtube.com/watch?v=hKiwgF6ojow&feature=related; on the second anniversary of the Hariri assassination, February 14, 2007: http://www.youtube.com/watch?v=q-lAMozBHeA&feature=related; on the tent city in downtown Beirut: http://www.youtube.com/watch?v=bFdQAmcWr-Y&feature=related.

5. In the summer of 2006, Israel attacked Lebanon for thirty-three days (July 12–August 14). Although Israel claimed that its bombs targeted only Hizballah strongholds, this military maneuver resulted in the destruction of civilian infrastructures such as the airport, ports, highways and bridges, water and sewage treatment plants, power and fuel stations, and private homes. Lebanon's Higher Relief Council estimated that one-fourth of the Lebanese population was displaced and more than one thousand civilians were killed. For more details on this topic, see the MIT *Electronic Journal of Middle East Studies* Summer 2006 special issue (Khalili 2006; Fattouh and Kolb 2006) or Hersh 2006.

6. For examples, see: http://electronicintifada.net/v2/article6178.shtml; http://electronicintifada.net/v2/article5400.shtml; http://samidoun.blogspot.com; the Siege of Lebanon blog: http://siegeoflebanon.blogspot.com/; Lebanon updates blog: http://electronicintifada.net/lebanon/.

7. http://www.lebanonsolidarity.org.

8. For a comprehensive critique of *New York Times* coverage of the 2006 war, see Munif 2006.

9. See his blog at: seigeoflebanon.blogpost.com, Saturday, September 9, 2006.

10. For more on this debate, go to: http://www.bbc.co.uk/blogs/worldhave yoursay/2006/08/everyones a winner.html.

11. Samidoon, International Solidarity Movement, the Civil Resistance Campaign, and Muwatinoon are among the groups who used Ta'-Marbouta as a meeting site after the Israeli attack on Lebanon in 2006.

BIBLIOGRAPHY

ABDULAH, HASSAN AL-

1993 *The First Real Estate Invasion: The Rebuilding of the City Center* [*Al-Ḥamlah al-ʿAqarya al-ula: Iʿadat Binaʾ wasat al-Madina*]. Beirut: Dar al-Jadid. (In Arabic.)

ABEDI, MEHDI, AND MICHAEL FISCHER

1993 "Thinking Public Sphere in Arabic and Persian." *Public Culture* 6: 220–230.

ABU-FAKHIR, SAQR

2002 Cultural Cafés: Beirut and the Emergence of Literary Modernity [Al-Maqahi al-Thaqafiya: Beirut, Intilaq Mawjat al-Ḥadatha al-Adabia]." *Al-Quds al-Arabia*, July 15, 2002. (In Arabic.)

ABU-KHALIL, ASAD

1985 "Druze, Sunni, and Shiʿite Political Leadership in Present-Day Lebanon." *Arab Studies Quarterly* 7(4): 28–58.

ABU-LUGHOD, LILA

1989 "Zones of Theory in the Anthropology of the Arab World." *Annual Review of Anthropology* 18: 267–306.

1991 "Writing against Culture." In *Recapturing Anthropology: Working in the Present*, ed. Richard Fox, 137–162. Santa Fe, NM: School of American Research Press.

ACCAD, EVELYNE

1989 "Feminist Perspectives on the War in Lebanon." *Women's Studies International Forum* 12(1): 91–95.

1990 *Sexuality and War: Literary Masks of the Middle East.* New York: New York University Press.

ADNAN, ETEL

1998a "Letter from Lebanon: Lebanon Loses What the War Did Not Destroy." *Al-Jadid Magazine* 4(24). http://leb.net/~aljadid/features/0424adnan .html.

1998b *Sitt Marie Rose: A Novel.* Trans. Georgina Kleege. Sausalito, CA: Post Apollo Press.

ADONIS

1985 *The Book of Siege* [*Kitab al-Hisar*]. Beirut: Dar al-Adab. (In Arabic.)

AKARLI, ENGIN

1993   *The Long Peace: Ottoman Lebanon, 1861–1920.* Berkeley: University of California Press.

ALAMEDDINE, RABIH

1998   *Koolaids: The Art of War.* New York: Picador USA.

ALONSO, ANA MARIA

1994   "The Politics of Space, Time, and Substance: State Formation, Nationalism, and Ethnicity." *Annual Review of Anthropology* 23: 379–405.

ALSAYYAD, NEZAR

1992   "Urbanism and the Dominance Equation: Reflections on Colonialism and National Identity." In *Forms of Dominance: On the Architecture and Urbanism of the Colonial Enterprise,* ed. Nezar Al-Sayyed, 1–26. Aldershot, Hants, UK; Brookfield, VT: Avebury.

ALTORKI, SORAYA, AND CAMILLIA FAWZI EL-SOLH

1988   *Arab Women in the Field: Studying Your Own Society.* Syracuse, NY: Syracuse University Press.

APPADURAI, ARJUN

1986   "Theory in Anthropology: Center and Periphery." *Comparative Studies in Society and History* 28(2): 356–361.

ASAD, TALAL

1994   "Ethnographic Representation, Statistics and Modern Power." *Social Research* 61(1): 55–88.

ʿAZMEH, ʿAZIZ AL-

1987   *Heritage between Authority and History* [*Al-Turath bayna al-sulṭan wa-al-tarikh*]. Casablanca, Morocco: Dar al-ʿUyun. (In Arabic.)

BARAK, OREN

2001   "Commemorating Malikiyya: Political Myth, Multiethnic Identity and the Making of the Lebanese Army." *History & Memory* 13(1): 60–84.

BARAKAT, HODA

1995   *The Stone of Laughter.* Trans. Sophie Bennet. New York: Interlink Books.

BASIL, JOSEPH

1994   "The First Conference on Popular Culture in Lebanon [Al-Muʿtamar al-Awal Hawala al-Thaqafa al-Shaʿbiya fi Lubnan]." *Al-Fikr al-Arabi* 3(77): 99–145. (In Arabic.)

BENHABIB, SEYLA

1997   "Models of Public Space: Hannah Arendt, the Liberal Tradition, and Jurgen Habermass." *The Feminist Review* 57: 4–27.

BERLINER, DAVID

2005   "The Abuses of Memory: Reflections on the Memory Boom in Anthropology." *Anthropological Quarterly* 78(1): 197–211.

BEYDOUN, AHMAD

1999   *The Shattered Republic: The Fate of Lebanon after Taif Accord* [*Al-Jumhuriya*

al-Mutaqaṭeʿa: Maṣaʾir al-Sigha al-Lubnaniya Baʿda Itfaq al-Taʾef]. Beirut: Dar Annahar. (In Arabic.)

BEYHUM, NABIL

1996 *Reconstruction and the Public Good: In Construction and the City* [*Al-Iʿmar wa al-Maṣlahah al-ʾAmmah: Fi al-ʿAmarah wa al-Madina*]. Beirut: Muʾassasat Al-Abhath Al-Madiniyah: Dar Al-Jadid.

BEYHUM, NABIL, ASSEM SALAM, AND JAD TABET, EDS.

1994 *Beyrouth: Construire l'avenir, reconstruire le passé?* Beirut: Dossiers de l'Urban Research Institute.

BISSAT, LAMIA EL-MOUBAYED

2002 "The Role of Civil Society in Rural Community Development: Two Case Studies from Lebanon." A Report for the ESCWA–World Bank Capacity Building Workshop on Rural Development in the Middle East, June 3–6, 2002, UN-House-Beirut. http://www1.worldbank.org/wbiep/decentralization/menalib/bissat.pdf.

BLANFORD, NICHOLAS

2006 *Killing Mr. Lebanon: The Assassination of Rafik Hariri and Its Impact on the Middle East.* London: I. B. Tauris.

BOU-HABIB, LINA

1998 "The Use and Abuse of Female Domestic Workers from Sri Lanka in Lebanon." *Gender and Development* 6(1): 52–56.

BOURDIEU, PIERRE

1979 *Algeria 1960.* Trans. Richard Nice. Cambridge: Cambridge University Press.

BOYARIN, JONATHAN

1994 "Space, Time, and the Politics of Memory." In *Remapping Memory: The Politics of TimeSpace*, ed. Jonathan Boyarin, 1–37. Minneapolis: University of Minnesota Press.

BRYCE, JENNIFER, NEFF WALKER, ET AL.

1989 "Life Experiences, Response Styles, and Mental Health among Mothers and Children in Beirut, Lebanon." *Social Science and Medicine* 28(7): 685–695.

CAMERON, STUART, AND JON COAFFEE

2005 "Art, Gentrification, and Regeneration—From Artists as Pioneer to Public Arts." *European Journal of Housing Policy* 5(1): 39–58.

CHARIF, HASSAN

1994 "Regional Development and Integration." In *Peace for Lebanon: From War to Reconstruction*, ed. Deidre Collings, 151–162. Boulder: Lynne Rienner Publishers.

CHEIKHO, LOUIS

1993 [1926] *Beirut Its History and Our Heritage* [*Bayrut Tarikhuha wa Atharuha*]. Beirut: Manshourat Dar al-Mashreq. (In Arabic.)

COLE, JENNIFER

1998 "The Work of Memory in Madagascar." *American Ethnologist* 25(4): 610–633.

COOKE, MIRIAM

1988 *War's Other Voices: Women Writers on the Lebanese Civil War.* Cambridge: Cambridge University Press.

1997 *Women and the War Story.* Berkeley: University of California Press.

CORM, GEORGES

1994 "The Politics of Reconstruction of the Second Republic [Al-Siyasa al-E'marya Lil Jomhuriya al-Thaniya]." *'Aba'd: A Journal of Lebanese and Arab Studies* 2 (October/November): 18–29. (In Arabic.)

1996 *Reconstruction and the Public Good: In the Postwar Economy and Politics [Al-I'mar Wa al-Maslahah al-'Ammah Fi Iqtisad Ma Ba'ada al-Harb Wa-Siyasatuha].* Beirut: Mu'assasat Al-Abhath Al-Madiniyah and Dar Al-Jadid. (In Arabic.)

DAGHER, CAROLE

2000 *Bring Down the Walls: Lebanon's Postwar Challenge.* New York: St. Martin's Press.

DAIF, RASHID AL-

1999 *Dear Mr. Kawabata.* Trans. Paul Starkey. London: Quart Books.

DAJANI, NABIL

1994 "The Role of the Mass Media in the Popular Participation to the Reconstruction of the Central District Area of Beirut." In *Beyrouth: Construire l'avenir, reconstruire le passé?* ed. Nabil Beyhum, Assem Salam, and Jad Tabet, 206–211. Beirut: Dossiers de l'Urban Research Institute.

DANIEL, VALENTINE

1996 *Charred Lullabies: Chapters in an Anthropology of Violence.* Princeton: Princeton University Press.

DARWISH, MAHMUD

1995 *Memory for Forgetfulness: August, Beirut, 1982.* Trans. Ibrahim Muhawi. Berkeley: University of California Press.

DAVEY, PETER

2000 "Beirut Planning Battles." *The Architectural Review* 207(1235): 20–21.

DAVIE, MICHAEL

1987 "Maps and the Historical Topography of Beirut." *Berytus* 35: 141–164.

1998 "The Emerging Urban Landscape of Lebanon." A paper presented at a conference entitled "A Conference on Lebanon in the 21st Century." Villanova University, PA, October 2–3, 1998.

DE CERTEAU, MICHEL

1988 *The Practice of Everyday Life.* Berkeley: University of California Press.

DEEB, LARA

2005 "Living Ashura in Lebanon: Mourning Transformed to Sacrifice." *Comparative Studies of South Asia, Africa and the Middle East* 25(1): 122–137.

2006   *An Enchanted Modern: Gender and Public Piety in Shi'i Lebanon.* Princeton and Oxford: Princeton University Press.

DENOEUX, GUILAIN

1993   *Urban Unrest in the Middle East: A Comparative Study of Informal Networks in Egypt, Iran, and Lebanon.* Albany: State University of New York Press.

DIRECTORATE GENERAL OF ANTIQUITIES OF LEBANON

1995   *Urban Archaeology 94: Excavations in the Souk Area of Downtown Beirut.* Beirut: Ministry of Culture and Higher Education, Directorate General of Antiquities, American University of Beirut, and Solidere.

DNAWI, ADNAN

1994   *Solidere: Speculation or Reconstruction Company?* [*Solidere: Mudaraba Amm Sharika 'aqarya?*]. Beirut: N. p. (In Arabic.)

DWAYHI, SHAWQI

2005   *Beirut's Popular Coffeehouses 1950–1990* [*Maqahi Beirut al-Shabeya 1950–1990*]. Beirut: Dar Annahar. (In Arabic.)

EICKELMAN, DALE

1998   *The Middle East and Central Asia: An Anthropological Approach.* Upper Saddle River, NJ: Prentice Hall.

ESCOBAR, ARTURO

2001   "Culture Sits in Places: Reflections on Globalism and Subaltern Strategies of Localization." *Political Geography* 20(2): 139–174.

FAOUR, ALI

1990   *Beirut, 1975–1990: Demographic, Social, and Economic Transformations* [*Bayrut 1975–1990: Al-Tahwulat al-Demoghraphiya wa al-Ijtimae'ya wa al-Iqtisadeya*]. Beirut: Geographic Institute. (In Arabic.)

FATTOUH, BASSAM, AND JOACHIM KOLB

2006   "The Outlook for Economic Reconstruction in Lebanon after the 2006 War." *The MIT Electronic Journal of Middle East Studies* 6: 96–114.

FAWAZ, LEILA

1993   *An Occasion for War: Civil Conflict in Lebanon and Damascus in 1860.* Berkeley: University of California Press.

FAWAZZ, MONA

2006   "Beirut: The City as Body Politic." *ISIM Review* 17: 22–23.

FELDMAN, ALLEN

1995   "Ethnographic States of Emergency." In *Fieldwork Under Fire: Contemporary Studies of Violence and Survival,* ed. Carolyn Nordstrom and Antonius Robben, 224–252. Berkeley: University of California Press.

FISK, ROBERT

1990   *Pity the Nation.* London: Andre Deutsch.

2005   "The Killing of Mr. Lebanon." *Washington Report on Middle East Affairs* 24, no. 3 (April): 10–12.

FOUCAULT, MICHEL

1977a *Discipline and Punish: The Birth of the Prison.* Translated from the French by Alan Sheridan. New York: Pantheon.

1977b [1963] *Language, Countermemory, Practice: Selected Essays and Interviews.* Trans. Donald Bouchard and Sherry Simon; ed. Donald Bouchard. Ithaca: Cornell University Press.

1980 *Power/Knowledge: Selected Interviews and Other Writings 1972–1977.* Ed. Colin Gordon. New York: Pantheon.

1986 "Of Other Spaces." *Diacritics* 16(1): 22–27.

FRASER, NANCY

1992 "Rethinking the Public Sphere: A Contribution to the Critique of Actually Existing Democracy." In *Habermas and the Public Sphere*, ed. Craig Calhoun, 109–142. Cambridge: MIT Press.

GAVIN, ANGUS, AND RAMEZ MALUF

1996 *Beirut Reborn: The Restoration and Development of Central District.* London: Academy Editions.

GENBERG, DANIEL

2002 "Public Space Inside Out: Beirut's Private and Public Spaces under Construction." In *Contesting "Good" Governance: Crosscultural Perspectives on Representation, Accountability, and Public Space*, ed. Eva Poluha and Mona Rosendahl, 237–269. London: Routledge.

GHANNAM, FARHA

2002 *Remaking the Modern: Space, Relocation, and the Politics of Identity in Global Cairo.* Berkeley: University of California Press.

GHOUSSOUB, MAY

1998 *Leaving Beirut: Women and the Wars Within.* London: Saqi Books.

GIDDENS, ANTHONY

1987 *The Nation-State and Violence.* Berkeley: University of California Press.

GILSENAN, MICHAEL

1982 *Recognizing Islam: Religion and Society in the Modern Arab World.* New York: Pantheon.

1996 *Lords of the Lebanese Merchants: Violence and Narrative in an Arab Society.* Berkeley and Los Angeles: University of California Press.

GUSTAFSON, PER

2001 "Meanings of Place: Everyday Experience and Theoretical Conceptualizations." *Journal of Environmental Psychology* 21(1): 5–16.

HADDAD, REEM

1999 "Mona's Mission . . . Reem Haddad Reports on the Fight to Save Beirut's Old Houses from Being Demolished." *New Internationalist* (August). http://findarticles.com/p/articles/mi_moJQP/is_315/ai_30493155.

HADDAD, SIMON

2002 "The Relevance of Political Trust in Postwar Lebanon." *Citizenship Studies* 6(2): 201–218.

HAGE, RAWI

2006   *De Niro's Game*. Toronto: House of Anansi Press.

HAKIMIAN, SUZY

1994   "Beyrouth: L'Histoire d'une Destruction, ou les Destructions de l'historie." In *Beyrouth: Construire l'avenir, reconstruire le passé?* ed. Nabil Beyhum, Assem Salam, and Jad Tabet, 17–29. Beirut: Dossiers de L'urban Research Institute.

HALBWACHS, MAURICE

1992   *On Collective Memory*. Ed. Lewis Cosser. Chicago: University of Chicago Press.

HANSSEN, JENS

2005   *Fin de Siècle Beirut: The Making of an Ottoman Provincial Capital*. London: Oxford University Press.

HARB, MONA EL-KAK

2001   "Urban Governance in Post-War Beirut: Resources, Negotiations, and Contestations in the Elyssar Project." In *Capital Cities: Ethnographies of Urban Governance in the Middle East*, ed. Seteney Shami, 111–133. Toronto: Toronto University Press.

HARRIS, WILLIAM W.

2005   "Bashar al-Assad's Lebanon Gamble." *Middle East Quarterly* 12(3): 33–44.

2007   "Crisis in the Levant: Lebanon at Risk?" *Mediterranean Quarterly* 18(2): 37–60.

HARVEY, DAVID

1989   *The Urban Experience*. Baltimore: Johns Hopkins University Press.

HAUGBOLLE, SUNE

2005   "Public and Private Memory of the Lebanese Civil War." *Comparative Studies of South Asia, Africa and the Middle East* 25(1): 191–203.

HEALEY, PATSY

2004   "The Treatment of Space and Place in the New Strategic Spatial Planning in Europe." *International Journal of Urban and Regional Research* 28(1): 45–67.

HERSH, SEYMOUR M.

2006   "Watching Lebanon: Washington's Interest in Israel's War." *The New Yorker* August 21. http://www.newyorker.com/archive/2006/08/21/060 821fa_fact?printable=true.

HOLSTON, JAMES

1989   *The Modernist City: An Anthropological Critique of Brasilia*. Chicago: University of Chicago Press.

HUYSSEN, ANDREAS

2000   "Present Pasts: Media, Politics, Amnesia." *Public Culture* 12(1): 21–38.

ITANI, MUKHATAR, AND ABDL LATIF FAKHOURI

1996   *Our Beirut [Bayrutuna]*. Beirut: Dar al-Anis. (In Arabic.)

JARKAS, RIYAD

1996   *Beirut in the Heart [Bayrout Fi al-Bal]*. London: Dar al-Rayyis. (In Arabic.)

JOHNSON, MICHAEL

1986   *Class and Client in Beirut: The Sunni Muslim Community and the Lebanese State 1840–1985*. Ithaca, NY: Ithaca Press.

JONES, DELMOS

1995   "Anthropology and the Oppressed: A Reflection on Native Anthropology." *National Association for the Practice of Anthropology Bulletin* 16(1): 58–70.

JOSEPH, SUAD

1988   "Feminization, Familism, Self, and Politics: Research as a Mughtaribi." In *Arab Women in the Field: Studying Your Own Society*, ed. Soraya Altorki and Camillia Fawzi el-Solh, 25–48. Syracuse, NY: Syracuse University Press.

2000   "Civic Myths, Citizenship, and Gender in Lebanon." In *Gender and Citizenship in the Middle East*, ed. Suad Joseph, 107–136. Syracuse, NY: Syracuse University Press.

JUREIDINI, RAY, AND NAYLA MOUKARBEL

2004   "Female Sri Lankan Domestic Workers in Lebanon: A Case of 'Contract Slaver'?" *Journal of Ethnic and Migration Studies* 30(4): 581–607.

KABBANI, OUSAMA

1996   "Postwar Reconstruction of Beirut Central District and the Experience of Solidere." A conference on the construction of the Mediterranean city, University of Venice, April 26–27, 1996.

KANAFANI, AFAF

1998   *Nadia, Captive of Hope: Memoir of an Arab Woman*. Armonk, NY: M. E. Sharpe.

KHALAF, SAMIR

1993   *Beirut Reclaimed: Reflections on Urban Design and the Reconstruction of Civility*. Beirut: Dar Annahar.

1994   "Culture, Collective Memory, and the Restoration of Civility." In *Peace for Lebanon? From War to Reconstruction*, ed. D. Collings, 273–285. Boulder, Colorado: Lynne Rienner.

2006   *Heart of Beirut: Reclaiming the Bourj*. London: Saqi Books.

KHALAF, SAMIR, AND GUILIAN DENOEUX

1988   "Urban Networks and Political Conflict in Lebanon." In *Lebanon: A History of Conflict and Consensus*, ed. Nadim Shehadi and Dana Haffar-Mills, 181–200. London: I. B. Tauris.

KHALAF, SAMIR, AND PHILIP KHOURY, EDS.

1993   *Recovering Beirut: Urban Design and Post-War Reconstruction*. Leiden, The Netherlands: E. J. Brill.

KHALAF, SAMIR, AND PER KONGSTAD

1973 *Hamra of Beirut: A Case of Rapid Urbanization.* Social, Economic, and Political Studies of the Middle East, vol. 6. Leiden, The Netherlands: E. J. Brill.

KHALILI, LALEH

2005 "Places of Memory and Mourning: Palestinian Commemoration in the Refugee Camps of Lebanon." *Comparative Studies of South Asia, Africa and the Middle East* 25(1): 30–45.

2006 "The Refugees Who Give Refuge." *The MIT Electronic Journal of Middle East Studies* 6: 57–67.

KHATIB, NASIMAH AL-

1993 *Beirut the Heritage [Beirut Al-Turath].* Beirut: Sharikat al-Matbu'at. (In Arabic.)

KHOURI, RAMI

2007 "A Carnival in Beirut," *Newsweek*, January 24. http://pewforum.org/news/display.php?NewsID=12515.

KHOURY, ELIAS

1990 *City Gates [Abwab al-Madina].* Beirut: Dar al-Adab. (In Arabic.)

1995 "The Memory of the City." *Grand Street* 14 (Fall): 137–142.

KHURI, FUAD

1975 *From Village to Suburb: Order and Change in Beirut.* Chicago: University of Chicago Press.

KING, ANTHONY D.

1992 "Rethinking Colonialism: An Epilogue." In *Forms of Dominance: On the Architecture and Urbanism of the Colonial Enterprise*, ed. Nezar Alsayyed, 339–355. Aldershot, Hants, UK; Brookfield, VT: Avebury.

KING, DIANE, AND KIRSTIN SCHEID

2006 "Anthropology in Beirut." *Anthropology News* 47(6): 40.

KOVATS-BERNAT, J. CHRISTOPHER

2002 "Negotiating Dangerous Fields: Pragmatic Strategies for Fieldwork amid Violence and Terror." *American Anthropologist* 104(1): 208–222.

KURAYYIM, MUHAMMAD

2005 *Beirut, You Are in Our Minds [Fil al-Bal ya Bayrut].* Beirut: Al-Dar al-Arabiya. (In Arabic.)

LABAKI, BOUTROS

1993 Development Policy in Lebanon, Between Past and Future." *The Beirut Review* 6 (Fall): 97–111. http://www.lcps-lebanon.org/pub/breview/br6/labakibr6pt1.html.

LEBANESE MINISTRY OF THE DISPLACED, THE

1996 *Return of the Displaced in Lebanon.* The City Summit, Istanbul, Turkey, June 3–14, 1996.

LEFEBVRE, HENRI

1996 (1968)   "The Right to the City." In *Writings on Cities*, ed. Eleonore Kofman and Elizabeth Lebas, 63–177. Oxford: Blackwell.

LOW, SETHA

1994   "Cultural Conservation of Place." In Conserving Culture: A New Discourse on Heritage, ed. Mary Hufford, 129–152. Urbana: University of Illinois Press.

1996   "The Power of Place." *Critique of Anthropology* 16(1): 57–62. A special issue edited by Ida Susser.

LOWENTHAL, DAVID

1998   *The Heritage Crusade and the Spoils of History.* Cambridge, UK, and New York: Cambridge University Press.

MACHNOUK, MOHAMAD

1994   *Beirut: Morning Beauty.* Beirut: Masters Publication Communication.

MAKDISI, JEAN SAID

1990   *Beirut Fragments: A War Memoir.* New York: Persea Books.

MAKDISI, SAMIR

1977   "Postwar Economic Development and a Look to the Future." *The Middle East Journal* 31(3): 267–280.

MAKDISI, SAREE

1997   "Laying Claim to Beirut: Urban Narrative and Spatial Identity in the Age of Solidere." *Critical Inquiry* 23(3): 660–705.

MAKDISI, USSAMA

2000   *The Culture of Sectarianism: Community, History, and Violence in Nineteenth-Century Ottoman Lebanon.* Berkeley: University of California Press.

MAKHZOUMI, JALA, AND REEM ZAKO

2007   "The Beirut Dozen: Traditional Domestic Garden as Spatial and Cultural Mediator." Published by the Proceedings of the Sixth International Space and Syntax Symposium, Istanbul, Turkey.

MALKKI, LIISA H.

1997   *Purity and Exile: Violence, Memory, and National Cosmology among Hutu Refugees in Tanzania.* Chicago: University of Chicago Press.

MARTIN, VANESSA

1997   "Illusions of the City." *Journal of Urban History* 23 (September): 760–769.

MASSEY, DOREEN

1993   "Politics and Space/Time." In *Place and the Politics of Identity*, ed. Michael Keith and Steve Pile, 139–159. London: Routledge.

1994   *Space, Place, and Gender.* Minneapolis: University of Minnesota Press.

MCDONOGH, GARY

1993   "The Geography of Emptiness." In *The Cultural Meaning of Urban Space*, ed. Robert Rotenberg and Gary McDonogh, 3–15. Westport, CT: Bergin and Garvey.

MILES, MALCOLM

1997   *Art, Space and the City: Public Art and Urban Futures.* London: Routledge.

MITCHELL, DON

2003   *The Right to the City: Social Justice and the Fight for Public Space.* New York and London: Guilford Press.

MITCHELL, TIMOTHY

1988   *Colonising Egypt.* Berkeley: University of California Press.

MULLINGS, LEITH

1987   *Cities of the United States: Case Studies in Urban Anthropology.* New York: Columbia University Press.

MUNIF, YASSER

2006   "Media Is the Continuation of War with Other Means: The New York Times Coverage of the Israeli War on Lebanon." *The MIT Electronic Journal of Middle East Studies* 6: 126–140.

MURNO, JOHN

1987   "Reconstructing Beirut: An Historical Perspective of the City." In *The Middle East City: Ancient Traditions Confront a Modern World*, ed. Abdulaziz Y. Saqqaf, 254–299. New York: Paragon House.

NAJEM, TOM PIERRE

2000   *Lebanon's Renaissance: The Political Economy of Reconstruction.* Ithaca, NY: Ithaca Press.

NARAYAN, KIRIN

1993   "How Native Is a 'Native Anthropologist'?" *American Anthropologist* 95(3): 671–686.

NASIR, AMJAD

1996   *Flapping the Wings: A Biography of Cities, Cafés and Journeys* [*Khabṭu al-ajniḥah: Sirat al-mudun wa-al-maqahi wa-al-raḥil*]. London: Riyad al-Rayyis Books. (In Arabic.)

NASR, SALIM

1993   "New Social Realities and Post-War Lebanon." In *Recovering Beirut: Urban Design and Post-War Reconstruction*, ed. Samir Khalaf and Philip Khoury, 63–80. Leiden, The Netherlands: E. J. Brill.

NASSAR, JAMAL

1995   "Sectarian Political Cultures: The Case of Lebanon." *The Muslim World* 85(3–4): 246–265.

NEDZI, LUCIEN N.

2006   "Lebanon's Contemporary Significance." *Mediterranean Quarterly* 17(4): 1–12.

NORA, PIERRE

1989   "Between Memory and History: Les Lieux de Memoire." *Representations* 26: 7–24.

NORTON, AUGUSTUS RICHARD

1987   *Amal and the Shi'a: Struggle for the Soul of Lebanon.* Modern Middle East Series, No. 13. Austin: University of Texas Press.

2000   "Lebanon's Malaise." *Survival* 42(4): 35–50.

PAERREGAARD, KARSTEN

2002   "The Resonance of Fieldwork: Ethnographers, Informants and the Creation of Anthropological Knowledge." *Social Anthropology* 10: 319–334.

PELEIKIS, ANJA

2001   "Shifting Identities, Reconstructing Boundaries: The Case of a Multi-Confessional Locality in Post-War Lebanon." *Die Welt des Islams* 41(3): 400–429.

PERCY, CHARLES

1995   "United States' Participation in the Economic Recovery of Lebanon." *Mediterranean Quarterly* 6(2): 1–16.

PETEET, JULIE

1996   "From Refugees to Minority: Palestinians in Post-War Lebanon." *Middle East Report* 200 (July–September): 27–30.

1997   "Identity Crisis: Palestinians in Post-War Lebanon." U.S. Committee on Refugees, World Refugee Survey, 34–39. Washington, D.C.

2005   *Landscape of Hope and Despair: Palestinian Refugee Camps.* Philadelphia: University of Pennsylvania Press.

PICARD, ELIZABETH

1996   *Lebanon, a Shattered Country: Myths and Realities of the Wars in Lebanon.* Trans. Franklin Philip. New York: Holmes and Meier Publishers.

PRED, ALLAN

1984   "Place as Historically Contingent Process: Structuration and the Time-Geography of Becoming Places." *Annals of the Association of American Geographers* 74(2): 279–297.

RAGETTE, FRIEDRICH

1980   *Architecture in Lebanon: The Lebanese House during the 18th and 19th Centuries.* Delmar, NY: Caravan Books.

RBEIZ, KAMAL JURJI

1986   *Oh, for Those Old Days, Beirut* [*Rizq Allah 'ala Hadik al-Ayyam Ya Ras Beirut*]. Beirut: Al-Matbouaat al-Musawarah. (In Arabic.)

RIBEIRO, GUSTAVO L.

1989   "The Constitution of Real Estate Capital and Production of Built-up Space in Rio de Janeiro, 1870–1930." *International Journal of Urban and Regional Research* 13: 47–67.

1994   *Transnational Capitalism and Hydropolitics in Argentina: The Yacyreta High Dam.* Gainesville: University Press of Florida.

RIFAI, ABD AL-JABBAR

2001   *Dialectic of Heritage in Contemporary Times* [*Jadal al-turath wa-al-'asr*]. Damascus: Dar al-Fikr. (In Arabic.)

ROWE, PETER, AND HASHIM SARKIS

1998   *Projecting Beirut: Episodes in the Construction and Reconstruction of a Modern City*. Munich and New York: Prestel.

SAGHIEH, HAZEM

2005   "Syria and Lebanon: Keeping in the Family." December 14. http://www .opendemocracy.net/conflict-middle_east_politics/syria_lebanon_3121 .jsp.

SAID, EDWARD

1993   *Culture and Imperialism*. 1st ed. New York: Knopf.

SALAM, ASSEM

1970   "City Planning in Beirut and Its Outskirts." In *Beirut: Crossroads of Cultures*, ed. Salwa Nassar, 167–184. Cultural Resources in Lebanon Series. Beirut: Librairie du Liban.

1998   "The Role of Government in Shaping the Built Environment." In *Projecting Beirut: Episodes in the Construction and Reconstruction of a Modern City*, ed. Peter Rowe and Hashim Sarkis, 122–134: Munich and New York: Prestel.

SALAM, NAWAF

1988   "Religious Communities in Lebanon; Les communautes religieuses au Liban." *Social Compass* 35(4): 455–464.

SALIBA, ROBERT

2000   "The Emerging Trends in Urbanism: The Beirut Post-War Experience." A paper presented at Diwan al-Mimar on April 20, 2000, Center for the Study of the Built Environment, Amman, Jordan. http://www.csbe.org/ Saliba-Diwan/essay1.htm.

2004   *Beirut City Center Recovery: The Foch-Allenby and Etoile Conservation Area*. Gottingern, Steidl, and London: Thames and Hudson Distributor.

SALIBI, KAMAL

1988   *A House of Many Mansions*. Berkeley: University of California Press.

SAMMAN, GHADA AL-

1997   *Beirut Nightmares*. Trans. Nancy N. Roberts. London: Quartet Books.

SARKIS, HISHAM

1993   "Territorial Claims: Architecture and Postwar Attitudes in the Built Environment." In *Recovering Beirut: Urban Design and Post-War Reconstruction*, ed. Samir Khalaf and Philip Khoury, 101–126. Leiden, The Netherlands: E. J. Brill.

SAWALHA, ASEEL

2003   "Healing the Wounds of the War: Placing the War-Displaced in Postwar Beirut." In *Wounded Cities: Destruction and Reconstruction in a Globalized World*, ed. Jane Schneider and Ida Susser, 271–290. London: Berg.

SAYIGH, ROSEMARY

1994   *Too Many Enemies*. London and New Jersey: Zed Books.

SEEDEN, HELGA

1993 "Lebanon's Archaeological Heritage." *The Beirut Review* 4 (Spring): 1–9.

SHADID, ANTHONY

2006 "Crisis Intensifies in Lebanon as Hezbollah Takes to Streets." *Washington Post Foreign Service,* December 2, A01. http://www.washingtonpost .com/wp-dyn/content/article/2006/12/01/AR2006120100129_pf.html.

SHARARAH, WADDAH

1985 *The Suspended City [Al-Madina al-Mawqufa].* Beirut: Dar al-Matbouat al-Sharqeyyeh. (In Arabic.)

SHAYKH, HANAN

1995 *Beirut Blues.* Trans. Catherine Cobham. New York: Anchor Books.

SHEHADEH, LAMIA RUSTUM

1999 *Women and War in Lebanon.* Gainesville: University Press of Florida.

SIBAI, ABLA, ASTRID FLETCHER, AND HAROUTUNE ARMENIAN

2001 "Variations in the Impact of Long-term Wartime Stressors on Mortality among the Middle-Aged and Older Population in Beirut, Lebanon, 1983–1993." *American Journal of Epidemiology* 154(2): 128–137.

SLACKMAN, MICHAEL

2007 "Rival Groups Kept Apart at Hariri Memorial in Beirut." *New York Times,* February 15. http://www.nytimes.com/2007/02/15/world/middleeast/15 lebanon.html?_r=1.

SLUKA, JEFFREY

2000 *Death Squad: An Anthropology of State Terror.* Philadelphia: University of Pennsylvania Press.

SOJA, EDWARD W.

1989 *Postmodern Geographies: The Reassertion of Space in Critical Social Theory.* London and New York: Verso.

SOLUTIONS GROUP (SARL)

1997 *Beirut in Motion.* Ed. IDAL. Beirut: Solutions Group SARL.

SULEIMAN, JABER

1999 "The Current Political, Organizational, and Security Situation in Palestinian Refugee Camps of Lebanon." *Journal of Palestine Studies* 29(1): 66–80.

TABET, JAD

1993 "Towards a Master Plan for Post-War Lebanon." In *Recovering Beirut: Urban Design and Post-War Reconstruction,* ed. Samir Khalaf and Philip Khoury, 81–100. Leiden, The Netherlands: E. J. Brill.

1994 "Methodology of Reconstruction: International Comparisons." In *Beyrouth: Construire l'avenir, reconstruire le passé?* ed. Nabil Beyhum, Assem Salam, and Jad Tabet, 79–85. Beirut: Dossiers de l'Urban Research Institute. (In French.)

1996 *Reconstruction and the Public Good. Heritage and Modernity: The City of War and a Memory for the Future [Al-I'mar Wa al-Maslahah al-'Ammah Fi al-Turath Wa al-Ḥadathah: Madinat al-Ḥarb Wa-Thakirat al-Mustaqbal]*. Beirut: Mu'assasat al-Abhath al-Madiniyah and Dar al-Jadid. (In Arabic.)

TAHAN, MOHAMMAD

1993   "Reading the Heritage: The Open Text and the Closed Text [Qira'at al-turath: Al-Nass al-Maftouḥ wa al-Nas al-Mughlaq]." *Al-Mustaqbal al-Arabi* 1(85): 34–51. (In Arabic.)

TARABISHI, GEORGE

1991   *Arab Intellectuals and the Heritage: A Psychoanalysis of a Collective Crisis [Al-Muthaqafun al-'Arab wa-al-Turath: Al-Taḥlil al-Nafsi li-'Uṣab Jama'i]*. London: Rayyes Books.

1993   *The Annihilation of Heritage in Contemporary Arab Culture [Mathhbahat al-turath fi al-thaqafah al-'Arabiyah al-mu'aṣirah]*. London: Saqi Books.

2000   *From Renaissance to Decline: The Crisis of Arab Culture in the Era of Globalization [Min al-nahḍah ila al-riddah: Tamazzuqat al-thaqafah al-'Arabiyah fi 'aṣr al-'awlama]*. Beirut: Saqi Books.

THOMPSON, ELIZABETH

2000   *Colonial Citizens: Republican Rights, Paternal Privilege in French Syria and Lebanon*. New York: Columbia University Press.

2003   "Public and Private in Middle Eastern Women's History." *Journal of Women's History* 15(1): 52–69.

TIESDELL, STEVEN, TANER OC, AND TIM HEATH

1996   *Revitalizing Historic Urban Quarters*. Oxford: Architectural Press.

TILLEY, CHRISTOPHER Y.

1994   *A Phenomenology of Landscape: Places, Paths, and Monuments*. Oxford, UK, and Providence, RI: Berg.

TIRAWI, AYMAN

2004   *Beirut's Memory; Dhakirat Bayrut; Mémoire du Beyrouth*. Beirut: Ayman Tirawi.

TRABOULSI, FAWAZ

1984   *A Wish That Will Never Come True: June–October 1982 ['Ala Amal la Shifaa Minhu: Ḥuzayran-Tishreen 1982]*. Beirut: Muasasat Al-Bahth Al-Arabiya. (In Arabic.)

1994   "The Role of War in State and Society Transformation: The Lebanese Case." Paper presented at a workshop entitled "War as a Source of State and Social Transformation in the Middle East," Paris, November 2–4, 1994.

2007   *History of Modern Lebanon*. London and Ann Arbor, MI: Pluto Press.

TRAD, ANDRE

2005   "The Legacy of Modern Architecture in Beirut, 1950–1975." *Worldview: Perspectives on Architecture and Urbanism from Around the World*, ed. Gregory Wessner, Architectural League *Worldview* coordinator and editor. http://worldviewcities.org/beirut/legacy.html.

TRENDLE, GILES

1991 "A Civil War Over Rebuilding Beirut." *Middle East Journal* 22: 19–20.

TURNER, VICTOR

1967 *The Forest of Symbols: Aspects of Ndembu Ritual.* Ithaca, NY: Cornell University Press.

UNITED NATIONS

1948 *The Universal Declaration of Human Rights.* http://www.un.org/Overview/rights.html#a12.

USSAYRAN, LAYLA

1996 *A Bird from the Moon: A Story about Beirut* [*Tair Mina Al-Qamar: Qisa ʿan Bayrut*]. Beirut: Dar AnnNahar. (In Arabic.)

VAN DUSEN, ROXANN A.

1976 "The Study of Women in the Middle East: Some Thoughts." *Middle East Studies Association Bulletin* 10 (May): 2–22.

VLOEBERGHS, WARD

2008 "The Genesis of a Mosque: Negotiating Sacred Space in Downtown Beirut." EUO Working Papers RSCAS 2008/17, Mediterranean Programme Series. Badia Fiesolana, Italy: European University Institute.

WAKIM, NAJAH

1998 *The Black Hands* [*Al-Ayadi al-Sud*]. Beirut: Sharikat al-Matbuʿat lil-Atawziʿ wa-al-Nashr. (In Arabic.)

WERBNER, RICHARD, ED.

1998 *Memory and the Postcolony: African Anthropology and the Critique of Power.* London: Zed Books.

WILLIAMS, RAYMOND

1989 *The Politics of Modernism: Against the New Conformists.* London: Verso.

WILSON, ELIZABETH

1991 *The Sphinx in the City: Urban Life, the Control of Disorder, and Women.* Berkeley: University of California Press.

WRIGHT, GWENDOLYN

1991 *Politics of Design in French Colonial Urbanism.* Chicago: University of Chicago Press.

YEOH, BRENDA S. A.

1996 *Contesting Space: Power Relations and the Urban Built Environment in Colonial Singapore.* New York, Kuala Lumpur, and Singapore: Oxford University Press.

YIFTACHEL, OREN

1995 "The Dark Side of Modernism: Planning as Control of an Ethnic Minority." In *Postmodern Cities and Spaces*, ed. Sophie Watson and Katherine Gibson, 216–242. Malden, MA: Blackwell.

Audi Foundation, 145n3
Australia, 109
authenticity, 40–43, 57, 80, 145n4. *See also* legitimacy
Awqaf, 29
Ayata Ashaab, 139
'Ayn el-Mreisse, neighborhood, 4, 84; Amal in, 59–60, 120–121; author and, 17–18; boundaries of, 62–63; displacement to, 38, 110–111, 120, 126; fishermen in, 62, 69, 71–72, 145n2; history of, 8, 53–55, 57, 61, 77; and Mosque Committee of 'Ayn el-Mreisse, 73–74, 78; power hierarchy in, 57–58, 60, 63–64, 87, 105, 145n14, 145n15; preservation of, 78–82; reconstruction of, 3, 10, 51, 60, 67; Solidere in, 57–59
'Ayn el-Mreisse Fishing Port, 72
'Azmeh, 'Aziz al-, 145n4

balad, 142n10. *See* Central District, of Beirut
Balla, Eskandar, 31–32
Basil, Joseph, 41–42
Baydoun, 142n9
BCD. *See* Central District, of Beirut
Beirut, Lebanon, 142n10, 146n6; architectural history of, 33–35; attacks on, 133, 137–139; author in, 7–9, 14–21, 141n1 (chap. 1); and Beirut Theater Collective, 10, 55, 69, 83–84, 86–87; and cafés, 92–96, 99, 105–106, 146n3, 146n11; and civil war, 1–3, 31, 34–35, 41, 90, 107, 109, 133, 146n8, 147n6; East Beirut, 12, 19, 86, 98, 110, 126; expresso vans in, 102–105; and fishing ports, 72; funeral homes in, 100–102; and heritage, 36–44; immigration to, 34, 108–110, 117–118, 125, 143n17, 144n2, 147n1, 147n10; and memory, 10–11, 29–36, 46, 96–97; and mili-

tias, 2, 24, 32, 35, 144n10, 145n14; and narratives of destruction, 31–32; nostalgia for, 12, 35, 72, 93; Old Beirut, 72, 79, 80, 142n3; prewar, 55, 89–90, 143n14; protests in, 133–136, 139–140, 148n2; reconstruction of, 4–5, 13–14, 23, 26–29, 48–49, 51, 53, 108, 111–112, 140, 143n16; and space, 47, 89, 91–92, 97–98; traditional dress in, 80, 82; West Beirut, 12, 54, 98, 147n3. *See also* 'Ayn el-Mreisse, neighborhood; Central District, of Beirut; displaced, the; government, Lebanese; Municipality of Beirut; reconstruction, of Beirut; Solidere; Southern Suburb of Beirut
Beirut Heritage Association, 145n3
Beirut Theater, 55; Committee, 10; struggle to maintain, 69, 83–84, 86–87
Benhabib, Seyla, 91
Berri, Nabih, 44
Beyhum, Nabil, 60, 118
Blanford, Nicholas, 148n1
Bliss Street, 63
bombings, of Beirut, 33; Israeli, 133, 136–137, 139, 147n2
Borj Ḥammoud, neighborhood, 18, 121
Bou-Habib, Lina, 147n13
Bourdieu, Pierre, 91
Brazil, 141n3
Bryce, Jennifer, 146n8
Bshirī area, 42

cafés: City Café, 96; Dolce Vita, 94; Express Café, 94, 96; French-style, 89, 92; and gender, 94–96; Horseshoe Café, 93–94, 96; Modca Café, 92–95, 137, 146n4; prewar, 92–95; Taʿ-Marbouta, 136–140, 149n11; Wimpy Café, 93. *See also* coffeehouses

Cairo, Egypt, 19, 86. *See also* Egypt

Canada, 109

CDR. *See* Council for Development and Reconstruction

Cedar Revolution, 133, 148n2

census. *See* statistics

Central District, of Beirut: civil war in, 35; destruction of, 29–30; and Horizon 2000, 27; politics surrounding, 134–136; and protests, 133–134; reconstruction of, 2, 23, 26, 39, 107, 133; Solidere in, 25, 44, 49, 51, 141n1 (intro)

Central Fund for the Displaced, 10, 116; and displaced persons, 128–129, 132; and evictions, 119, 122; responsibilities of, 112, 131, 147n10

Chamoun, Camille, 34, 143n15

checkpoints, 98, 144n5, 145n9

Christians: and displaced persons, 65, 110, 114, 147n4, 147n9; and division of Beirut, 12, 26, 59, 63, 98, 109, 121; Greek Orthodox, 39–40, 63, 147n4; Maronite, 40, 110, 134, 147n4, 147n9; population of, in Lebanon, 19; and preservation of Beirut, 40–42, 78, 134

Chūf Mountains, 41, 109, 110

Civil Resistance Campaign, 136, 149n11

civil war, Lebanese, 110, 139; coffeehouses during, 146n3; effect of, on Beirut, 1, 31, 133, 147n6; government during, 24; history of, 34–35, 41, 90, 146n8

Clemenceau Street, 33, 63

coffee: and expresso vans, 97, 102–105; and funeral homes, 82, 89, 97, 100–102, 105; and social act of drinking, 4, 18, 71, 89

coffeehouses: al-Farouq, 99; al-Ghalayini, 99; al-Ḥaj Dawood, 99; *al-maqha*, 93, 99; al-Qazaz, 99;

Falasteen, 99; and gender issues, 91–92, 146n3; and history, 94–96, 106, 146n11; as public space, 4, 87, 89

Cole, Jennifer, 97

collective(s), 69, 87, 105; action, 78; amnesia, 41, 105; experience, 96; heritage, 42; identity, 108; immigration, 34, 108–109, 117–118, 144n2, 147n1; memory/memories, 1, 12, 46, 80, 83, 96–97; pat, 87; remembering, 30, 82, 87, 96–97; responses, 67; space, 94; vision, 41. *See also* Beirut Theater

colonization, 10–11, 34

compensation, for the displaced, 128; abuse of, 113, 115–117, 119–123; and eviction, 109, 126–127; government and, 112–113, 118–119, 129, 141n2, 147n6; negotiations for, 5, 8, 51, 65–67, 124, 130, 132, 147n3

contractors, 122, 137

Cooke, Miriam, 146n8

Corniche Street, 72; and boundaries of 'Ayn el-Mreisse, 52, 54, 55, 62; and coffee shops, 103–105

Council for Development and Reconstruction (CDR), 9, 33

Cultural Dialogue Circle, 145n3

cyberspace. *See* Internet

Dagher, Carole, 142n1

Dar al-Mreisse. *See* 'Ayn el-Mreisse

Davie, Michael, 33–34, 145n1

de Certeau, Michel, 10

demonstrations, political. *See* protests, political

Denoeux, Guilian, 143n14

developers. *See* investors

Dimitryous II, 31–32

displaced, the, 4–5, 25; Amal Movement and, 59–60, 65, 84, 147n3, 148n12; attitudes toward, 7, 107–

building of Beirut, 13, 26–29, 34–35, 51, 143n16; and services, 24–25, 64, 70, 104; and Solidere, 7, 38, 109

Green Line, 12–13, 19, 98, 141n4, 144n14, 146n9

Haddad, Reem, 144nn3–4
Haddad, S., 144n4
Hakimian, Suzy, 30
Halbwachs, Maurice, 97
Ḥammam al-Askari, neighborhood, 72
Hamra District, neighborhood, 8, 105, 136, 146n5
Hamra Street, 92–95, 99, 102, 136–137
Hanssen, Jens, 143n12
Harb, Mona, 144n10
Hard Rock Cafe, 54, 84; and Mosque Committee of ʿAyn el-Mreisse, 4, 73–74, 76–78, 87; opening of, 60
Hariri, Rafik, 142n8 (chap. 2); assassination of, 76, 104, 133–134, 139, 148n1, 148n4; as businessman, 27, 60, 72–73, 128, 131, 148n3; government of, 24–25, 40, 107, 122–123, 142n2; and plan to rebuild, 26–28, 31–32, 44, 46, 77, 140; and Solidere, 2, 31–32, 39, 131, 141n1 (intro). *See also* government, Lebanese
Hariri, Saad, 135
Hariri Foundation, 40
Ḥay Līf, 119
heritage, Lebanese: in ʿAyn el-Mreisse, 69, 71–72, 78, 80–83, 87; debates about, 2, 40–44, 145n4; the displaced and, 118; preservation of, 14, 23, 27–30, 36, 38, 143n11, 145n3
Hersh, Seymour M., 148n5
Higher Relief Council, 148n5
Hizballah, 10; and Beirut theater, 83; control of Beirut by, 39, 52, 57–58,

134–135; and displaced population, 65, 147n3, 148n12; war of, with Israel, 133, 148n5
Holiday Inn, 77
Horizon 2000, 27
house, traditional Beiruti, 53, 143n11, 144n3
House of the Lebanese Craftsman, 54, 144n6
housing: alternative, 8, 51, 115, 131; and cultural meaning, 46; and the displaced, 60, 63, 110, 113, 118; and immigration, 34; negotiations for, 129–132
ḥusayniyah, 147n12
Huyssen, Andreas, 83

identity, collective, 42, 108. *See also* collective(s): immigration; memory
immigration, 34, 108–109, 117–118, 144n2, 147n1
India, 147n13
International Industrial Exhibit Maʿarad al-Sinaʿat al-Dawli, 45
International Solidarity Movement, 149n11
Internet, 5, 90, 135–136
investors, 108, 128, 144n2; in ʿAyn el-Mreisse, 8, 60, 69–70, 73, 78, 83, 144n6; Beiruti opinions about, 52–53, 118; and the displaced, 51, 65–66, 111, 118, 130; and Hariri government, 27, 46; and reconstruction of Beirut, 13, 38, 48, 57–58, 144n10; and Solidere, 25, 28, 131
Islamic Group, 38, 143n19
Israel: attacks on Lebanon, 47, 60, 84, 109, 111, 125, 133, 135, 137–139, 147n2, 148nn5,13, 149n11; occupation of Palestine by, 34, 46; relationship of, with Lebanon, 136, 146n6

Johnson, Michael, 148n15
Jones, Delmos, 141n5
Joseph, Suad, 18
Jumblat, Kamal, 142n1
Jumblat, Walid, 147n9
Jureidini, Ray, 147n13

Kabani, Ousama, 36
Kabbani, Mohamad, 43
Khalaf, Samir, 26, 143n14, 146n5
khliw, 65–66, 112
Khoury, Elias, 30
Khuri, Fuad, 64, 147n1
King, Diane, 142n7 (chap. 1)
Kongstad, Per, 146n5
Kurds, 63

Labaki, Boutros, 143n15
Lahoud, Emile, 142n2
landlords: and developers, 8, 126; and
    the displaced, 4, 107–109, 124;
    interviews with, 20; and Shi'ite
    groups, 65; tensions with tenants,
    3, 65–67, 78
Lebanese Intifada. *See* Cedar
    Revolution
Lebanese University, 17, 114
Lebanon, 28, 147n13; author's diffi-
    culties in, 14–16; coffeehouses in,
    89–96, 103; the displaced in, 113,
    118, 125, 127, 147n4; ethnoreligious
    groups of, 2, 39, 40, 42, 141n6,
    144n13; government of, 27, 143n15,
    146n6; history of, 33–34, 41, 53,
    143n9, 144n4; Israeli occupation
    of, 84, 135–136, 139, 147n2, 148n13,
    148nn5–6, 149n9, 149n11; migra-
    tion to, 34, 147n1; politics in, 19,
    133–135, 138–139; South Lebanon,
    109, 121, 125, 128, 138, 147n2. *See also*
    Beirut, Lebanon; displaced, the;
    government, Lebanese; *and indi-
    vidual neighborhoods*

Lefebvre, Henri, 11
legitimacy: debates about, 57; and the
    displaced, 114, 117, 122, 124, 126; of
    Lebanese government, 2, 107, 128
"let's wait and see" attitude, 3, 5, 65–
    66, 124
Līf, Ḥay, neighborhood, 119
liminality, 14, 94, 107, 128, 132; of
    the displaced, 115, 117. *See also*
    uncertainty
Low, Setha, 46
Lowenthal, David, 40

Machnouk, 142n9
madina, 142n4
Makdisi, U., 143n9
Makhzoumi, Jala, 144n3
Malkki, Liisa, 117–118
Maluf, Ramez, 27
maps: of 'Ayn el-Mreisse, 51, 60–63,
    145n1; destroyed, 19; Solidere,
    47–48
March 14th Coalition, 134–135
Martin, Vanessa, 27
Martínez Street, 55, 77
Martyrs' Square, 134
Masri, Rania, 136
McDonogh, Gary, 47
media, 137; and cafés, 94–96; and the
    displaced, 118–119; electronic, 135–
    136; and Lebanese government,
    44, 148n2; and protests, 135; tele-
    vision, 24, 27, 72, 134, 136, 148n3
Mediterranean Sea, 8, 62, 144n6
memory, 1, 19, 23; of 'Ayn el-Mreisse,
    64, 78, 80–83, 87; and cafés, 93,
    96–97; collective, 30, 42, 46, 83,
    96–97; and connection to place,
    3, 4, 11–12, 14, 29, 71, 89, 125, 127;
    cultural, 42, 83; of downtown Bei-
    rut, 30; and history, 87; politics
    of, 12, 45; and power relationships,
    14, 25; of prewar era, 45, 89–92;

displaced and, 90, 109; media, 148n2

Universal Declaration of Human Rights, 131

urban planning, 11, 14, 46, 115

urban rights, 3, 11, 15, 51

Ussayran, Layla, 103

violence: and the displaced, 118, 119, 121; and uncertainty, 111; wartime, 83, 125

Vloeberghs, Ward, 142n3

Wadi Abu Jmīl, 36, 119–120

Wakim, Najah, 123

wasaṭ al-balad, 20. *See also* Central District, of Beirut

Web sites. *See* Internet

Werbner, Richard, 97

West Beirut. *See* Beirut, Lebanon: West Beirut

women: anthropologists, 17, 142n8; in cafés, 4, 93–96, 105, 138; and gendered space, 18, 55, 84, 90–92, 98, 99–102, 104, 146n9; and fieldwork, 17; and memory, 90–91, 96–97; and protests/war, 105, 134, 146n8

Workers' Union of Lebanon, 70

World Bank, 27

World War I, 33

Yatim, Hussein Ali, 43

Yiftachel, Orean, 46

Zako, Reem, 144n3

Ziadeh, Niqola, 90

Zqaq el-Blāṭ, neighborhood, 7

CPSIA information can be obtained
at www.ICGtesting.com
Printed in the USA
FSHW011836030821
83629FS